ASK ME WHAT'S FOR DINNER ONE MORE TIME

ALSO BY MEREDITH MASONY

Scoop the Poop

ASK ME WHAT'S FOR DINNER ONE MORE TIME

INAPPROPRIATE THOUGHTS ON MOTHERHOOD

MEREDITH MASONY

GALLERY BOOKS

New York London Toronto Sydney New Delhi

Gallery Books
An Imprint of Simon & Schuster, Inc.
1230 Avenue of the Americas
New York, NY 10020

First Gallery Books trade paperback edition September 2020

Photographs courtesy of the author.
Illustrations by Jeff Garczewski. Illustration@punkbyte.com.

Manufactured in the United States of America

10 9 8 7 6 5 4 3 2 1

Library of Congress Cataloging-in-Publication Data

Names: Masony, Meredith, author.
Title: Ask Me What's for Dinner One More Time : inappropriate thoughts on motherhood / Meredith Masony.
Identifiers: LCCN 2020009916 (print) | LCCN 2020009917 (ebook) | ISBN 9781982117962 (paperback) | ISBN 9781982117979 (ebook)
Subjects: LCSH: Motherhood. | Work and family. | Motherhood—Humor. | Parenthood—Humor.
Classification: LCC HQ759 .M37147 2020 (print) | LCC HQ759 (ebook) | DDC 306.874/—dc23
LC record available at https://lccn.loc.gov/2020009916
LC ebook record available at https://lccn.loc.gov/2020009917

ISBN 978-1-9821-1796-2
ISBN 978-1-9821-1797-9 (ebook)

I dedicate this book to The Business Manager, aka my husband,
and my three delightful blessings: Matias, Sophia, and Brian.

Being a wife and mother is only part of who I am;
however, you will always have my entire heart.

Contents

CONTENTS

INTRODUCTION

Welcome to Inappropriate Thoughts on Motherhood

My name is Meredith, and I am an unfiltered mom who has inappropriate thoughts. What I mean by this is that I discuss the tough topics that arise from parenting, including but not limited to: smears on light switches, cracked nipples from breastfeeding, level-seven meltdowns in the Target toy aisle, hemorrhoids, where babies come from, the puberty, the smells related to the puberty, and so much more. I have three kids, one husband, and a dog who smells like a fish. Between working, doing 800 loads of laundry and dishes each day, and trying to and failing at keeping everyone happy, I am barely keeping it together. I don't believe in balance when it comes to work life and home life. I believe in making choices and finding perspective so that I can chase my dreams and keep my family from being the next set of contestants on *Naked and Afraid: Family Edition.* There are plenty of days that I never get out of my jam-jams, but I manage to get what needs to be done . . . done. I love connecting with women, moms, and wives on subjects ranging from potty training and breastfeeding to puberty and the sex talk. Making videos while venting about the daily grind—being the family maid, cook, errand runner, and car pooler, all while keeping my husband happy above and below the sheets—has been an amazing blessing for my family and has brought women seeking connection, commiseration, and a good laugh to my internet doorstep. To my delight, this community has become a beacon of hope for moms who need support, a good laugh, and honest relatability in the chaotic universe that is Motherhood.

In the fall of 2014, I was spending way too much time on Facebook. At first, I was amazed at how perfect all of my "real-life" friends were. I would scroll my newsfeed in complete and utter wonderment, thinking, "Holy crap! I had no idea my friends were so well put together. I mean, I see them at work and they are a complete disaster. Here on Facebook they have the most perfect lives."

I saw the perfect Caribbean vacation pictures, flawless family portraits, crisp craft projects, delicious home-cooked meals, and so much more. What had me audibly sighing in disbelief, even more than the Martha Stewart–inspired Thanksgiving cornucopias decorated with Papyrus decoupage, were the romantic sentiments and gestures from couples spewing love bombs at each other on their timelines.

> "To my greatest love, William. You are my everything. Each minute with you is magical and makes my heart skip a beat. You are the wind beneath my wings."
>
> —Susan

First of all, get outta here, Susan. No one loves anyone or anything that much. Okay, maybe I love wine that much, but COME ON! Who on earth says these things? Let's be honest, I've met William . . . and we have discussed the fact that he clips his toenails at the dinner table. The more time I spent online, the more I wondered if I was a failure (even if I knew William was no great catch). With so much perfection out there, where on earth did I fit in? If I had to measure up to these standards, it clearly meant I was failing at parenting, marriage, life in general, and of course, Papyrus decoupage.

I had no idea that at the age of 34, I would have the opportunity to be blessed with a tumor that would change my life. At the time, of course, I didn't think the tumor was a blessing. I was scared. I was alone in my head. I was wallowing in self-pity. However, realizing that I might die in my mid-30s, with three young children and a husband who would need some substantial help in the dating arena, forced me to put the proverbial pen to paper. I decided I couldn't take it anymore. I was going to get rid of the filter and write about all of the taboo topics of parenting: marriage, relationships, sex, you name it. I had been holding it in for so long and it was time to release the pressure. I let the words flow. The raw words. The tired words. The words that lived in my head that I was so scared to show anyone, let alone the internet. I shared the real side of parenting. The side that makes your brain hurt. The side that isn't camera-ready. The side that makes all of us feel inferior, like shells of ourselves. I wrote about the issues I faced with my children. I discussed my marriage, including the marriage bed.

I even wrote a post about my son's autism diagnosis before I had told my immediate family. I decided that it was important to let it all hang out. Like *really* hang out.

And slowly but surely, I started to get messages from women who were struggling just like I was. I wasn't alone after all. There were others out there on their own lonely desert islands, quietly tracing the letters *S.O.S.* in the spilled Cheerios on the kitchen floor at 6 A.M.

And then I started creating videos. I had never shot a video before in my life, but I knew that I needed to find another way to connect with my community. I started shooting video on my MacBook and watched a few YouTube clips, learning how to edit. My first videos were cringe-worthy to say the least, but I felt like the best way to connect to other moms was to show my face. My first viral video was "What Moms Actually Want for Mother's Day." My husband had left that week on a golf trip, and had the nerve to call me to see if he could stay a few more days, potentially missing Mother's Day. I was not impressed, and so I decided to shoot a video about the things I really wanted on Mother's Day. As a mom, I am on the clock 365 days a year, 24 hours a day, 7 days a week. I wanted a day off. Yup, a day off from butt wiping, snack making, laundry washing, cooking, cleaning, you name it. I wanted to sit by the pool and sip mimosas. I wanted to be taken to brunch, lunch, and dinner. I wanted to be left alone, and I wanted it to be quiet. It was amazing to watch how quickly people were reacting to the video. Women were tagging their husbands in the post and begging for a day off. Men were laughing, saying, "Don't you want to be with your kids?" The video was picked up by NBC, FOX, CBS, and several other networks. By Mother's Day, it had been viewed over 10 million times. I was in shock. My Facebook page, which had 3,000 followers at the beginning of May, now had over 60,000 followers. I knew I was on the right track.

I loved making videos. It was unbelievably freeing to cover topics like the realities of married sex, things you can say to your toddler and your drunk friend, taking a phone call when your kids are home, getting my kids to go to bed, and what's it like when a man has a cold, and people kept watching. These videos were either loved or hated, and it made me realize that people could relate to my struggles, because they were also struggling. They had a child who acted as though he had never been told to go to bed before. They had a husband who assumed death was imminent the second he sneezed. These women were my people. They got me. Like really fucking *got* me. To. The. Motherfucking core! My videos were shared, stolen, syndicated by news networks, and featured on the *Today* show, *GMA*, and *Morning Express* on HLN with Robin Meade. My Facebook page exploded to over 200,000 followers in that period of time. Two hundred thousand people who felt like I felt. Who cried in the closet at the end of the day. Who knew what it was like to be exhausted by motherhood, while conflicted with how much joy and love it also brought.

What started as a series of personal venting sessions has turned into a thriving community where women share their struggles as moms, wives, and career women; where they feel free to vent without judgment or shame; where they can feel like themselves again.

And that's what I want this book to do as well. I see it as a part of my mission to give you permission to be who you are. To be happy where you are in life. To remember that you are humans, not just wives and mothers. I want you to know that you are not alone. I want you to have a laugh and remember that raising humans is tough, and there will be days when we don't get it all done. In my opinion, *balance* is a four-letter word. Raising a family is about making choices and letting go of the bullshit. Be you. Own you. Love you. Your family will love you for it.

This book will bring you joy, laughter, and the knowledge that you really aren't alone. In fact, there are so many moms out there just like you. Moms who don't shower for days and can't stand wiping butts. I mean, I wipe my kids' butts, but why on earth should I enjoy it? No one wants to look at another person's anus and wipe it. Yet we do it for the love, and because we hate scrubbing lightning streaks out of undies.

So, you had a baby. Congratulations! You grew a human in your uterus, adopted, or received a bonus baby via marriage. Any way you slice it, you are a mom and now the shit is really going to hit the fan. There is no owner's manual. There are absolutely no instructions. You are out in the deep blue sea, attempting to stay afloat. There is no land in sight, and a fucking stork has dropped a baby into your arms and squawked, "Stay afloat, motherfucker, and while you're at it, raise that baby. Make sure to do it right. Don't fuck this up."

Motherhood is anything but appropriate. There are so many bodily fluids and decisions to be made. It is overwhelming, exhausting, and mind numbing at times. It will cause you to say WTF more times than you would have thought humanly possible. However, it will also cause a rush of emotions that are so exhilarating and fulfilling that I can honestly say being a mom is the most humbling and joyous part of who I am. So let's get started, shall we?

Author's Note

Because I am a product of the '80s, and my favorite books were volumes of the *Encyclopaedia Britannica*, we need a glossary of terms to understand what the fuck is going on in our parenting journey. A journey that is sure to be fraught with shit storms and joyous moments, most of which are totally out of our control.

Hot Mess Mom: A mom who is doing her best but probably falling short. She tries her hardest, but life has slapped her in the face today and she needs a do-over. She may or may not have taken a shower this week, a fact she is well aware of, so you don't have to comment on the smell. She is probably wearing a pair of yoga pants, a messy bun on the top of her head, and a T-shirt covered in what she hopes is chocolate and boogers. She loves her family with all her heart, but she is definitely going to complain and vent about being in the trenches of parenting. She has earned it. She grew humans and has the battle scars to prove it.

Filter-free parent: Someone who does not believe in putting a filter on every photo, every Facebook post, every Instagram story, or on her life, for that matter. A filter-free parent is open to discussing what life is really like in the trenches of parenting. She is real, raw, honest, and can find the humor in the daily struggles that parenting can present. Like that time I forgot to pick my kid up from school and I took a picture of the note the teacher left at the front desk—yeah, I posted that on Facebook for the world to see. I can't possibly be the only one who ever forgets her kid at school. I would have eventually remembered, I think.

Susan: My nemesis and yours. Susan is every parent who has given that side-eye glance to let you know she is a better person than you are. She is the mom who reminds everyone at the PTA meeting that at the last bake sale, you brought cookies that were processed at a facility where nuts and other allergens might be present. It's cool, Susan, we all know you are perfection—we just don't care.

Zero fucks to give: This one is kind of crystal clear. It means you really don't care—and aren't going to pretend to care. Now I get it, this seems like an impossible life philosophy to obtain, but I guarantee it is possible to get there. It took me about ten years of marriage and eight years of parenting three children under the age of eight, but for holy fuck's sake, I got there. If you need me to use it in the proper context, it would look like this: "Seriously, Susan, no one cares that you did a virgin-alpaca-hair-sewing bead set with your kids today. I mean, we've seen the pics on Instagram, and we obviously know your children weren't even involved in that craft project. We're not stupid."

Advice: This one is a bit tricky, because most of the time when someone asks for advice, she wants to know the best thing to do. I most likely will not be giving you the best advice. I am just being honest. My advice might be shit. Take it or leave it, this is all I have to give.

ASK ME WHAT'S FOR DINNER ONE MORE TIME

CHAPTER ONE

I Love My Children . . . I Love My Children: A Mother's Mantra

Have you ever walked into a bathroom and had to flush the toilet for a forgetful child? How about washing eight loads of laundry a day, where you are washing clothing that you know your child had on her body for two-tenths of a second and then decided it was time for a costume change because, rumor has it, she is up for an Emmy nomination in this year's "Toddler Drama" category? Did you sit down on a wet spot on the couch today? After you sat on that wet spot, did you bend down to smell it? You know you did. I bet it smelled like piss. When was the last time you stepped on a Lego?

Of course, we love our children, but that doesn't mean they don't annoy the crap out of us. I bet your kids do a lot of the same nonsense as mine, and I bet your response isn't so different from mine (maybe with less cursing). Let's take a look, shall we?

SNACKS, SNACKS, SNACKS . . . WHY YOU SHOULD BUY STOCK IN NABISCO WHEN YOU HAVE YOUR FIRST BABY

I love food, but I hate grocery shopping. I don't dislike the grocery store. I am at the grocery store at least twice a week. This is not an exaggeration, I promise you that. I make one trip on Sundays where I stock up on everything I need for school lunches, Sunday dinner, and meals with my codependent relatives (Eric, Trey, and their son Mason; we eat together four nights a week), and then I am usually back by Thursday. Thursday's shopping trip includes all the shit I forgot on Sunday and usually Preparation H hemorrhoid wipes. For some reason my hemorrhoids usually flare on the weekends, for obvious reasons.

I know I have a family of five and five people eat a lot, but why do my children eat this much? Who the hell needs to snack like this? I am pretty sure the reason I hate grocery shopping is because I know that the second I get home, my kids will grab 98 percent of what I purchased and eat it within five minutes of being home. And then in ten minutes they will come up to me and say, "Can I have a snack?"

FOR. THE. LOVE. The sentence "Can I have a snack?" makes my blood boil. Before having kids, I had no idea how much children ate. I mean, I really had no idea I would buy so much granola, Quaker Oats should sponsor me. I feel like someone should follow me around and when I am picking up the damn granola bar wrappers from between the couch cushions a voice-over actor should say, "This cleanup session was brought to you by Quaker Oats. Click the link for your coupon."

I spend so much money on fruit cups, yogurt, granola bars, crackers, and fruit. For the most part, my kids eat relatively healthy snacks, but after an apple, a granola bar, a bowl of Goldfish crackers, two string cheeses, and a Go-GURT, how on earth is their appetite not quenched? Seriously?? I need to know! How are they still hungry?

The best part is when I tell them that dinner is about 15 minutes away and they fall to the ground, exclaiming that they are going to starve to death. Really??? GIVE ME A BREAK, KID, YOU WILL NOT STARVE! Dinner arrives and they poke their fork at the pork chop on their plate and say, "I'm not really hungry." WHAT? WHAT DID YOU JUST SAY? Child, look at me! You are going to eat that entire pork chop or I can guarantee that the programming you just tuned in to is intended for mature audiences only and will end with a mother holding a flip-flop in one hand and her poor life choices in the other. Five minutes after dinner is done . . . "Can I have a snack?"

Before having children, I would have never thought that the word *snack* would elicit such a visceral reaction from my body. It is almost like being stabbed with a thousand needles all at once. Maybe you think that is a bit of an overreaction, but come back and let me know how you feel about the word *snack* after an eight-week summer vacation with three kids who you are positive have a six-foot tapeworm living inside their bellies.

Ten Things You Can Hear in Any Home on Any Given Day

Picture it: it's 2020 and you are a fruit fly on the wall of the home of some woman whose children also refused to eat a bunch of decaying bananas; you would most likely see and hear the following conversations.

1. What's for dinner? Spaghetti? We just had spaghetti. I don't want that again.

2. Why are you so mean?

3. Can I have a snack?

4. Where are my socks?

5. I'm bored. I have nothing to do.

6. You are always working. Why don't you spend time with me?

7. I don't want to do my homework.

8. I don't want to clean this up. I didn't make this mess.

9. Why can't I get a hamster?

10. He/She hit me!

My Reply to Ten Things I Hear in My Home on a Daily Basis

1. (*What I say*) Yes, we are having spaghetti again. It is cheap and fast, and due to the fact that I have to carpool three of you to soccer, piano, and gymnastics, this is what you get. Deal with it. (*What I want to say*) FOR FUCK'S SAKE! Be happy you are going to eat!

2. (*What I say*) I am mean because I am tired. I love you but I do not always like you, and guess what . . . I am your mom, not your friend. (*What I want to say*) FOR FUCK'S SAKE! I have always been mean. This is as good as it is going to get.

3. (*What I say*) STOP ASKING ME FOR SNACKS! ALL YOU DO IS ASK FOR SNACKS. HOW IS IT POSSIBLE THAT YOU ARE THIS HUNGRY ALL THE TIME? (*What I want to say*) FOR FUCK'S SAKE! NO MORE FUCKING SNACKS!

4. (*What I say*) Find your own damn socks. I am not the one who needs socks, so you better get looking. (*What I want to say*) FOR FUCK'S SAKE! GET YOUR SOCKS!!!!!

5. (*What I say*) There is plenty to do. We have windows to wash, bathrooms to clean (there is plenty of urine on the floor from where you missed the bowl), garbage to take out, laundry to fold . . . (*What I want to say*) FOR FUCK'S SAKE! There is plenty to do and I swear to all things holy, I can't take much more.

6. (*What I say*) I work because we have bills to pay. I work because the mortgage does not pay itself. I work because you have an addiction to snacks. I work because I love providing for this family. I am doing my best to spend as much time as I can with you. Can you give me some slack? (*What I want to say*) FOR FUCK'S SAKE! I wish we could pack up and move to a compound in a wooded area where we aren't required to pay bills or wash our clothing, but there hasn't been a casting call for that reality show yet, so I have to keep working to make sure we don't have to file for a second, yes I said second, bankruptcy.

7. (*What I say*) I don't want to do your homework either, but we both know that it needs to get done. (*What I want to say*) FOR FUCK'S SAKE! How do you have homework again? Are you planning on becoming a brain surgeon? If not, we need to talk to this teacher. Her expectations are a bit much for this family's endgame. College isn't for everyone.

8. (*What I say*) Guess who else didn't make this mess??? (*holding up both of my thumbs and pointing at myself with the enthusiasm of The Wiggles at a sold-out concert*) ME! And guess who always has to clean up everyone's messes??? ME! So, guess what? It is time for you to learn how to clean up and help me out. (*What I want to say*) FOR FUCK'S SAKE! And then everything else I stated above.

9. (*What I want to say*) Hamsters smell awful. Hamsters make a ton of noise. Hamsters are basically rats. Hamsters bite. Do I really need to continue with this list? NO HAMSTERS! (*What I say*) FOR FUCK'S SAKE! NO RATS IN THIS HOUSE! I AM NOT PICKING UP ANY MORE FECES!

10. (*What I say*) ARRRRGGGGGGG! FOR THE LOVE OF ALL THINGS HOLY! (*I bend down and take off my flip-flop.*) Are you here to tattle-tale??? (*What I want to say*) FOR FUCK'S SAKE! And once again, the same thing I said above.

I feel like I should get some credit for wanting to say "for fuck's sake" and not actually saying it. I mean, that shows some restraint, doesn't it? As a mom, our days are filled with these conversations over and over and over again. It is mind numbing, but life is full of repetition. If by the time my kids are 18 they can find and put on their socks and shoes, feed themselves, and aren't massive cunt weasels, I have done my job. I know, I know. That last word was a bit offensive, but I really don't want my kids to grow up and act like weasels.

I'M A YELLER, AND YOU SHOULD BE ONE TOO. HERE'S WHY.

I am aware that it is 2020 and each year new research comes out detailing how my parenting style is destroying my children's lives. I know, I am the worst. No matter what we do as parents, we can't win. One award-winning book tells you to sleep train; another book says if you do that you will raise anal-retentive children. Another book tells you to breastfeed until the child is five years old and that bottle feeding will guarantee that your child never goes to college. While yet another book will tell you that breastfeeding for too long will definitely cause an Oedipus complex. Not really, but you get what I'm saying.

I decided a few years ago that I have zero fucks to give. I decided that I was going to parent as I saw fit and I would leave the rest of the parents around the globe to do the same. And guess what? Our parenting styles can evolve over time. As our children grow and as we collect more children, we tend to learn what works and what doesn't. We tend to find a rhythm. We tend to go with our gut. And in my case, that means yelling. Yelling is part of my parenting style.

I am loud in general. I rarely start out yelling, but most days, I end with yelling. Do I yell because I enjoy it? you ask. No, I yell because I have three children who have a tendency to ignore me until I have lost every shred of my sanity.

A normal day starts out with me waking up the kids. First I walk into my youngest child's room and ask him to wake up. He usually rolls over and grunts. I then go into my daughter's room and pull the covers off her. She will reply with a shriek that can make the hair stand up on the back of your neck. My oldest child, the teenager, will say, "I'm up, I'm up," but that is just a tactic to get me to leave his room.

Obviously because it is a school day, they want to sleep in. I walk back into their rooms three minutes later for a second time, asking in a louder, more authoritative tone, "Please get up—we need to get moving." I will then head into the kitchen to do dishes or pack lunches. If my blessings have yet to rise from their slumber, I begin to yell. I shout, "Let's go! You need to get up or we are going to be late." First yell of the day usually happens before 8 A.M. Eastern Standard Time. I am not calling them names. I am not screaming obscenities, but I am yelling. Once I yell, like magic, their butts are out of bed and they are getting ready. I think I am going to stop calling it yelling, and start calling it "increased vocal directives."

I am not sure how my yelling is going to ruin my children, but I have been told by several researchers/experts and other parents on Facebook that I am, in fact, ruining their lives. Yet I stand by my parenting style. I have no intention of not raising my voice. Think about it: most people need to be motivated. As adults, we go to work because we are motivated by money. We need money to pay the bills, buy the food (you know, all the snacks our kids need to survive), and live our lives. We need motivation in order to thrive and succeed. I am simply motivating my children to brush their teeth, do their homework, eat their dinner, and clean up their rooms. I don't just yell because I love the sound of my shrill voice. Believe me, if they pick up their toys the first time I ask, I don't raise my voice. That hasn't happened yet, but I will keep you posted.

MOMS DON'T POOP IN PRIVATE

I have often thought about putting a stall in my bathroom. Yes, like a public bathroom stall. One with a lock and a full roll of toilet paper. You see, my bathroom is small, so the toilet is right next to the shower. There is only one door to the bathroom, so when you open it, you are looking directly at the toilet. In a public restroom, you at least get a stall, a wall, a divider, so that you can do your business in peace.

I haven't pooped in peace in about 14 years. I am a pretty quick pooper. I can usually be in and out in under three minutes. As efficient as I am, I miss being able to efficiently crap in private. I know what you are going to say: "Just lock the door, lady!" Believe me, I have thought about that, but I can't. I have three kids who are constantly asking for things, needing something, or on the verge of burning down my house. If I lock the door, they will just come bang on it to ask me where the scissors and matches are, and the incessant pounding really cramps my style when I am trying to evacuate my bowels. I finally gave up on locking the door after my daughter started screaming that she had cut her finger off and was bleeding to death on the other side. I jumped up, pre-wipe, mind you, to find her with a paper cut that had no visible blood trail.

I love some good solid eye contact when deep in conversation, but I am not a fan of talking to anyone while I am pooping. I don't know why anyone would want to talk to me while I am mid-drop, let alone be three feet from me, in the splash zone, so to speak. Yet my children have a desire, dare I say a need, to be with me while I poop.

What really gets me, though, is that no one wants to go into the bathroom when my husband is pooping. He doesn't lock the door either, but no one ventures into that path of destruction. He is not an efficient pooper, by the way; he is a "full lunch break" kind of pooper. He is usually crushing candy and scrolling Facebook, enjoying a nice, quiet poop. NO ONE BOTHERS HIM! NO ONE! Once, my son asked me for help with a math question and I said, "Go ask your father." He said, "No, he is in the bathroom." I said, "So, you always come in when I am in the bathroom." He looked at me and said, "Yeah, but do you know how bad Dad smells when he poops? I am not going in there." So basically, because my shit doesn't stink as bad as my husband's, I am the one who is punished. I am seriously considering eating more Taco Bell.

WHAT'S THAT SMELL? THE POOP, BLOOD, OR CHOCOLATE DILEMMA

When I was pregnant with my first child, I had awful morning sickness. I was sick for most of the day, and smells were always the thing that triggered my trips to the throne. I had no idea that smells would become such a big part of my life. I assumed that once the morning sickness passed, my smell issue would calm down and I would go back to normal. I was completely wrong. I could smell a block of cheese from a mile away. I'd always loved cheese, but when I got pregnant, I immediately hated the smell of Asiago cheese. Oddly enough, my husband found a new love for Asiago cheese and decided he needed to put it on everything he was going to eat. My ability to smell things, and my inability to tolerate smells, the smells my baby made, and then subsequent babies made, have filled the past 14 years of my life.

Think about it. As a mom, we have to smell all the smells. Not just our own smells, but everyone else's smells. The husband's smells, the kids' smells, the dog's smells, and don't forget about the lactose-intolerant neighbor kid who always likes to take a shit at your house—his smells too. As they say, everyone has their own brand, and I am the "aroma-chologist" of the family. Becoming a mom gave me the ability to smell things a mile away as well as determine which one of my kids farted. That's right, I can tell which one of my kids farted by the scent of their toot. I shall sniff this for the next 10 to 15 years, God willing my youngest decides to move out.

Once we have children, our world is taken over by odors. Do you remember the first time you found a bottle of spoiled milk in your car? FOR. THE. LOVE. The smell of six-day-old curdled milk can make people with a steel stomach retch uncontrollably, causing them to make the cat vomit face. If you don't know what the "cat vomit face" is, just think about a human coughing up a hairball, as a cat would, then insert the sound of a person on the verge of vomiting. You're welcome.

I don't know if curdled milk is the worst smell, but it is a pretty bad one. I once found a poopy diaper in my kids' toy bin. Not sure how many days it was in there, but let's just say we no longer have that bin—the smell would not leave. Not even a priest who studied exorcism could have helped us with that situation. I can see it now. The priest exclaims, "I demand you leave this place! Go back to the fires of hell where you came from. In the name of the Father, the Son, and the Holy Ghost!" He then begins to burn sage and throw holy water on the bin, his arms waving in an emotional plea to evacuate the smell of brimstone and split pea and ham baby food from the bin.

The worst is when you spend a few minutes sniffing to find the location of the smell and when you get to the spot, you find a smear. The smear could be poop, chocolate, or blood. At this point you most likely have a philosophical conundrum. Your life has led you to this point. What kind of mom allows her child to run around smearing poop, chocolate, or blood all over her home? EVERY MOM, that's who. You get a little closer, take a deeper sniff, and make an educated guess. DON'T EVER TOUCH OR LICK THE SMEAR. THAT IS A COMPLETE AMATEUR MOVE. IT IS ALMOST NEVER CHOCOLATE!

Let me tell you a little story about a time I found myself in this particular dilemma. It was early morning and I was screaming at the kids to get ready for school. I was washing my face and I grabbed my face towel to pat myself dry. As I brought the towel to my face I saw a streak of brown, and as I brought the towel closer, I recognized the scent. It was in fact feces. I was about two inches away from wiping my face with a shit-stained towel. One of my kids had either wiped their ass or their shit-covered hands with my face towel. WHAT IN THE ACTUAL FUCK? I was face to face with feces—or is it face to feces?—and it almost shattered my world. It also begged a few questions. Which one of my kids wiped shit on my face towel, and why? My kids had been potty trained for years at this point, yet the evidence was clear: there was poo-poo on my once white and fluffy "Mommy only" face towel. I spent most of the morning trying to figure out how my child wiped their ass, apparently toilet paperless, and then "washed" their hands and dried them off with my hand towel. How on earth did they leave the bathroom with shit on their hands and not realize it? I had failed as a mother. In my defense, it is actually super hard to teach another person to wipe their own ass.

The smells and smears, much like the feces-stained face towel we just discussed, of motherhood can be overwhelming, but they are part of the terrain. Moms can smell a dirty diaper across the house. Moms can smell snack-stealing kids who smuggled cookies into their rooms. Moms can smell it all, even when we don't want to.

BEDTIME . . . IT'S MERELY A SUGGESTION

Before having kids, I envisioned bedtime as a time to snuggle with my children and read their favorite bedtime stories. I would read the lines of each character in a different voice, and we would reminisce on how magical our day was. We would connect on a level that would make Lifetime movie producers call me to schedule production of a new made-for-TV movie, *Mythical Best Mom Ever Does Exist*, about my ability to be the best mom ever.

However, I am going to be completely honest here and tell you the truth. Are you ready? My favorite time of the day is bedtime, and not because of what I mentioned above. I love bedtime because it means my kids are going to sleep and they will be away from me. Like *far* away from me. Not touching me. Not talking to me. Not whispering with their hot breath in my ear, asking for the 900th snack of the day.

I love my children . . . I love my children . . . but by the end of the day, I am exhausted. Between work, kids, school projects, gymnastics practices, football, soccer, cleaning the house, laundry, and cooking dinner, I am so ready for bedtime. However, it seems that my children are never ready for bedtime. It seems that bedtime is merely a suggestion, which, obviously, it isn't. It feels like my kids have amnesia when the sun goes down. They look at me like they have never gone to bed before. They are convinced that I am attempting to ruin their lives, when in fact I simply want them to get some sleep. I have tried several approaches to bedtime. They include:

The Logical Approach

MOM: Children, it is time for bed. The CDC recommends an average of eight to ten hours of sleep for children your age. If you do not get this amount of sleep, you will not grow, function, or learn properly, leading to a lifetime of despair and eventually tragedy.

KIDS: WHAT DO YOU MEAN IT'S BEDTIME! WE DON'T WANT TO GO TO BED!

The Emotional Approach

MOM: Children, I love you. The sun rises and sets based on my utter love for you. It is time to have sweet, sweet dreams. Please lie down and I will sit here and pat your back until you have drifted into an amazing state of sleep that parallels a propofol-induced coma.

KIDS: WHAT DO YOU MEAN IT'S BEDTIME! WE DON'T WANT TO GO TO BED!

Bribery (Because It Happens) Approach

MOM: Children, I am at my wits' end. I will give you anything you ask for if you go the fuck to bed. I mean it. List your demands and it will happen.

KIDS: WHAT DO YOU MEAN IT'S BEDTIME! WE DON'T WANT TO GO TO BED!

Fear-Based Approach

MOM: Children, I AM DONE! That. Is. It! I have completely lost my shit. Everyone is going to bed. I swear to all things holy! If any one of you gets up out of your bed, I will explode. The sky will rain down with ash and fury and my ability to exist as we know it will cease. I will literally go insane.

KIDS: WHAT DO YOU MEAN IT'S BEDTIME! WE DON'T WANT TO GO TO BED!

No matter which approach you try, your children will attempt to get out of bed several times after you have put them to bed. At bedtime, children turn into dehydrated philosophers who need a hug. They have a million questions about the finality of life. They forgot that they ingested 47 juice boxes throughout the day and they desperately need a "sip" of water. Which is hilarious because if you offer them water throughout the day, they will look at you as though you are poisoning them. And the best is when you have just finished screaming like a lunatic and they look at you and say, "I just called you here because I needed a hug." Like, seriously, kid. You are a dick! You didn't want a hug. You wanted to get out of bed, which is where I am desperately trying to go!

Bedtime is a test of wills. Sometimes you win, sometimes you lose. No matter what, bedtime will come again tomorrow, and you will fight that same fight again.

BATH TIME IS AN AQUATIC EVENT . . . BRING YOUR RAIN BOOTS

In my home, we take showers. Only showers. First of all, let me explain my aversion to baths. Think about it. You fill a tub with hot water. You get into that water. You are dirty. You are now in the dirty hot water. You are now stewing in your own filth, creating people soup. Yup, people soup. I am not a fan of baths. My kids, on the other hand, loved taking baths, but that didn't stop me from banishing baths from my home.

Baths are just another way my kids avoid bedtime. See, bath time happens right before bedtime, and taking baths is a massive process. My kids know that filling the tub takes eight minutes. Then they throw every bath bomb we own into the tub, staining the tub a violent-diarrhea-brown color, which takes an additional 12 minutes. Next comes bath-time cleanup, which takes three minutes, because they do a super shitty job at cleaning up the bathroom. Finally, they come out and tell me they are done;

however, I then require them to take a shower because they in fact didn't wash their bodies with soap, or their hair with shampoo. They spent the majority of bath time pouring the body wash and shampoo down the drain, where most of my hopes and dreams live. This will undeniably tack on an additional 37 minutes of water time, prior to the bedtime process.

About four years ago my younger son, who was then six, was taking a bath. He had been in the bathroom for almost 30 minutes. I had checked on him a few times, but after calling his name three times, with no answer, I went back to see if he was finally finished. When I approached the bathroom, I looked down and saw water flowing under the door into the hallway. As I opened the door, the tub was overflowing and my six-year-old was riding a rubber duck pool float like he was in the movie *8 Seconds*, starring Luke Perry, who cinematically chronicles the life of Lane Frost, 1987 PRCA Bull Riding World Champion. I was a big fan of *90210*, and I watched anything Luke Perry was in; sue me. My son had gotten water, bubbles, shampoo, and soap all over every inch of the floor and the walls. He had been riding that duck for much longer than eight seconds.

I immediately began screaming like a lunatic, which was falling on deaf ears. My son seemed to be surprised that I was unhappy with the new indoor hot tub he'd created in the bathroom. I spent the next 30 minutes soaking up the floor and cleaning walls, while yelling about water waste and proper bath-time protocol. "Did you know we are in a drought? How on earth did it seem like a good idea to get the pool rafts and put them in the tub? Who told you to ride this raft like your life depended on it?" I went on and on until I realized something. We didn't have to do bath time. Everyone in this house was old enough to shower. It was at that time that I issued a decree across the land. *There shalt be no more baths taken in my kingdom. The Queen has spoken.* I still find my son, who is now ten, attempting to plug the tub while he is showering so he can perform scientific experiments with the tear-free shampoo, but we are firmly a shower-only family. Also, I bang on the door every time I hear the tub filling and scream like a lunatic, demanding that they "turn on the shower and pull that plug, or I swear to all that is holy, I will come in there and drain that tub like you've drained my soul."

WHY WE CAN'T HAVE NICE THINGS

In 1989, I was nine years old. I was visiting my grandparents' house in Florida, which is where most grandparents live. I know this because I have lived in Florida for over 30 years now, and we have all the old people, I promise. Anyway, my brother and I were running through the living room, and I tripped and fell over the coffee table and onto the couch. I remember the feeling of my face smacking into the couch cushion and sticking to the thick plastic cover. My face made an audible Velcro "RIIIIIIPPPPPPP" sound as I yanked my head back. I remember thinking that my grandparents were super weird. They had plastic covers over all of their furniture. They had a "formal" living room. We weren't allowed to go in there or touch anything in there. It was "off limits" to any of the kids, and if we were found in there, we got the wooden spoon. My grandmother was one of the most loving people on the planet, but if you pissed her off, she would chase after your ass wearing a housecoat, her hair in curlers, and either a wooden spoon or a flip-flop in her hand. You did not want to piss Babs off. Back to the story. I thought it was super weird that they put their furniture in plastic, like it was some kind of museum. Why would anyone do that?

Fast-forward 30 years and I know why those genius bastards did just that. Kids ruin everything. They simply do. They ruin the couch, the floors, the walls, the chairs, the blankets, the blinds, the kitchen utensils—you name it, they ruin it. My grandparents were simply trying to keep their chic 1980s floral furniture in its peak condition.

I own a brown couch that was once white. My couch is covered in a myriad of substances, including but not limited to maple syrup, grape juice, snot, Cheerio dust, crackers, and the remnants of a bowl of French onion soup that I could never really get out of the corner cushion. My kids have ruined so many of my things, the couch is just the tip of the iceberg. Much like the *Titanic*, any new or gently used items have been sunk and destroyed by my blessings.

Here is a brief list of items my children have broken/destroyed:

1. Laptop computer (Someone spilled a bottle of hair detangler all over it.)

2. Couch (We talked about this already. Lots and lots of fluids. Also my kids were playing super-secret Karate

Ninja a few summers ago, and jumped so hard they broke the springs. Now when you sit on it, you fall to the right side.)

3. Kitchen table (Mostly ruined by juice spills, food, pens, pencils, crayons, permanent marker, and some fluids. I have not had sex on my kitchen table. Just sayin'.)

4. Coffee table (Someone stood on it and broke one of the legs. Not sure who; the kids said "Not Me" did it.)

5. Window blinds (Almost every set of window blinds in my home is broken. They have pulled the strings so hard that they no longer move the blinds up or down. They also ripped off the rod that moves the blinds side to side. We can't put the blinds up or down. They simply sit there, serving no real purpose. Only one set remains in working use, and by the time this book is published, I am positive it will be broken as well.)

6. Remote control, aka clicker in our house (Every one of my kids has broken at least two clickers each. We have purchased more Apple TV remotes than I want to admit. If the kids weren't so quiet while watching TV, I would stop buying replacement remotes.)

7. My soul (I'm kidding . . . I'm kidding . . .)

So, you get the gist of it. Kids ruin and break everything. Some parenting experts say it's because they are new to the world, so they have to explore how things work. I say it's most likely due to the fact that they are assholes and they like to touch everything with deadly force. Maybe I will take a note from the late 1970s and my grandparents, and cover all of my furniture in plastic, creating a mausoleum-like appearance in my home. More likely, I will only shop at IKEA for new furniture until my kids grow up and move out.

THE PROBLEM WITH *AMERICAN IDOL* AND YOUTH SPORTS

All parents think that their child is special. We believe that our children will move mountains, and they just might. However, I can tell you as a former teacher, your child might be special to you, but is probably not the greatest thing since sliced bread. I'm super sorry to burst your bubble, but hear me out.

I love *American Idol*. I watched pretty much every episode until Katy Perry became a judge. I don't personally know Katy Perry, but I wasn't a fan of her critiques. They lacked something that only Paula Abdul could deliver. Paula, Randy Jackson (Dawg), and Simon Cowell will forever be my favorite set of musical talent show judges. I remember watching Kelly Clarkson when she won the first season. I was so invested, I felt like I had also won a singing competition. I was also 21 and knew nothing about the music industry or the ability to sing on pitch. Back to my point. My sincerest apologies.

When I first saw the show, it was simply entertainment. I loved seeing some of the singers succeed, while simultaneously secretly enjoyed watching others fail miserably. It was such a fun show. Fast-forward years later, which included marriage, the arrival of my delightful blessings, and a new perspective on life: *American Idol* was still on television and I was still a fan. However, my view on the show had shifted. I started watching the show from a mother's perspective. I would see these young contestants who could not sing a single note on key, and I would become embarrassed for them. I would want to jump in front of them to shield them from the camera. I would see them being interviewed side by side with their parents, and I would think, "How on earth did this mother think it would be a good idea to let this kid sing on national television? He can't sing!" Why would any mother not only allow her tone-deaf child to appear on this show but also cheer him on?

I know how harsh this sounds, I really do, but how is this beneficial to the child? As a mother, I know how important it is to nurture your child's dreams. We need to be an unwavering support to our children. We see the potential in them. We know that they are special, but are they *American Idol* special?

I did a quick Google search to find out that fewer than 5 percent of musicians ever make a reasonable living from their musical endeavors. I am not here to crush musical dreams, but deliver a dose of reality. Are we helping our children or hindering them when we enable a dream that has no hope of succeeding? When we enable a dream for our children that has no chance of success, we are forcing them to shoulder a massive burden of stress.

My daughter is a competitive gymnast. She was fourth overall in the nation for AAU gymnasts in 2019 in her age division. She is a good gymnast. She also loves to sing. She, like me, sings all day long. She, like me, cannot carry a tune in a bucket. She told me she wants to be on *American Idol* one day, and my momma heart sank. Do I tell her to work hard and maybe one day she will be on the show, or do I tell her that the only audience that would ever appreciate her voice would be the deaf community? Obviously I would never say that, but I did tell her, "Sweetie, I love you. You are great at a lot of things. You are an amazing gymnast. You are super smart. You are a hard worker. It is very hard to become a professional singer and only a small percent of the population will achieve that. You have many strengths, but singing isn't one of them. You can sing for me. You can sing in the shower. You can sing in the car, but I don't think *American Idol* is in your future." My daughter seemed unfazed by my words. As a parent, it is our job to crush some dreams. I know you may not agree with me on this, but it is one of the hardest parts of parenting, and it's important. Our job is to be there for our kids in their successes and failures, and to help them understand that they will not be successful at everything. No one is.

You can apply this to youth sports, academics, and any other activity your children become involved in. As parents, we travel a fine line between being supportive and becoming enablers. If we enable our children to believe that they are the best at everything, they will not be able to survive failure. Failure is so important. I have failed over and over again. Practice doesn't make anything perfect, but it makes it better, and we have to strive to be better each and every day. I love my children an indescribable amount. It might not sound like it after that last paragraph, but I am honest with them because I love them. I would be doing a massive disservice to my daughter if I told her to pursue a career in music and that she was the best singer to ever grace this earth. I mean, have you ever heard of Whitney Houston?

Our children will not all become professional athletes, professional singers, academic giants, or Nobel prize winners. Our job as parents is to raise good humans who are good to other humans. I will support and crush my children's dreams as necessary. I will show up each and every day, but I will not lie to my children. Life is hard enough; I will not set them up for failure. I would rather prepare them to learn from failure so they can find success.

TODDLERS AND DRUNK PEOPLE HAVE A LOT IN COMMON

If you are currently living with a toddler, you might experience some déjà vu. Living with toddlers is very similar to living in a college dorm room. You know what I'm talking about. You put all your food in the fridge, and five minutes later you find your roommate's spoon deep in your yogurt. Later that night, your drunken roommate walks into your room, asking for help taking off her shoes. Now that you are a parent, life with a toddler is pretty similar. Toddlers are messy. Toddlers are loud. Toddlers are assholes. Toddlers are basically drunk people. If you don't believe me, take a look at these 20 things you can say to both your toddler and a drunk friend.

1. *You can't nap here; you need to go to your bed.* Why is it that toddlers and drunk people can fall asleep anywhere? At 40, I can't seem to fall asleep in my own bed at my designated bedtime.

2. *We don't eat food from strangers.* Toddlers will take food from anyone, or anywhere for that matter. Toddlers will eat food off the floor, out of their car seat, or out of a dog's mouth. I once had a drunk friend eat a piece of pizza that had fallen cheese-side down on a street. An asphalt street.

3. *We never touch our private parts in public.* Toddlers love to touch their private parts. Especially toddler boys. I have also had to say, "We don't put our penises on the kitchen table." Luckily for toddlers, touching themselves in public won't lead to jail time, but drunk people, watch out! Take your pee-pee out in public and you will be spending the night in the clink.

4. *We pee in toilets, not in the street.* Toddlers love to pee wherever they please. For the most part, I am cool

with toddlers peeing on a tree or bush, but if we are walking into Target, it's really not cool to piss in front of the automatic doors. Drunk people really shouldn't pee in public, but at the end of the night, someone is always hiding behind a car, peeing. Been there, done that. Luckily I didn't end up in jail.

5. *Chew with your mouth closed.* Both toddlers and drunk people love to play the "see food" game. However, it isn't as much fun as they think it is.

6. *Keep your fingers out of your nose.* Let's be real. I still have to tell my 10- and 11-year-olds to keep their fingers out of their noses. Also, my husband. So, perhaps it isn't just the toddlers and drunk friends.

7. *I am not playing that song again. We have heard it 15 times.* Remember the "Baby Shark" craze of a few years ago? . . . Yeah, that is like a form of torture. Remember when your drunk friend wanted to listen to some awful love song while going through a breakup? Just as bad.

8. *Don't put that in your mouth.* Toddlers love to pretend to be coin-operated washing machines at the Laundromat. They eat quarters like it's their job. And those drunk friends, they can't be trusted to keep their mouths shut.

9. *It's not nice to stare.* Why is it that toddlers love to stare and point out the obvious? I know that they are learning about their surroundings and everything is

shiny and new and all, but FOR THE LOVE, can we please not talk about the overweight bald man who has an eye patch? I don't think he is a chubby pirate, I think he is an accountant who recently had an accident at the racquetball courts. Drunk friends are pretty much the same here. Like legit, same.

10. Yes, those are boobies, but we don't touch those. Boobies are apparently fun for everyone. Toddlers just like them because they provide food. Drunk friends want to see them escape like *Free Willy*.

11. I know, couch *is a funny word.* I have a lot of fond memories of when my toddlers began talking. They would butcher so many words, and it was awesome. "Am-ba-lance" and "pa-sketti" are two of my all-time favorites. Same goes for a drunk friend trying to order dinner at an Italian restaurant.

12. Stop looking at me like that. Disapproval runs rampant with toddlers and drunk friends. Why? Because no one likes to be told what to do.

13. I'm going to tell your father. Oh yes. I have said this a million times . . . to both my toddlers and drunk friends. We have to use a bit of fear in hopes they will make the right choice.

14. Please keep your hands to yourself. Toddlers and drunk friends are so incredibly handsy. They touch your face, they touch your hair, they touch the inside of your open eye. I guess they just need to explore with their tactile senses.

15. Do you really think whining will get you what you want? Yes, yes it does. Both toddlers and drunk friends will use this tactic to get exactly what they want. How aggravated and tired you are will most likely determine if they in fact get it.

16. Please hold my hand in the parking lot. I don't want you to get hit by a car. Toddlers and drunk friends are extremely dangerous in parking lots. They tend to run off without permission and they never look both ways.

17. I don't have any more money. Please stop asking. Toddlers and drunk friends are a very big drain on your bank account. They never seem to have any money to contribute to the dinner bill and they always want a late-night snack that they can't afford. They will also never pay you back.

18. Do you need to sit in my lap? Toddlers and drunk friends just need lots of love. They will most likely feel right at home in your lap, and although it might be a bit uncomfortable for you, it will make their day.

19. I need you to use nice words. Toddlers and drunk friends can get pretty mean. They love to use very specific harsh descriptive words, like *fat*, *giggly*, *smelly*, and *mean*. They can cut deep, like real deep.

20. Why are you holding yourself, do you need to pee? They definitely need to pee. Most potty-training toddlers and drunk friends will signal their need to use the restroom by holding themselves until they are directed to the closest toilet, or an accident occurs. Either way, you will be left to clean up the mess.

Luckily, we can use the same tactics to calm our toddlers and drunk friends. We can simply sing a song, give them a snack, and tuck them in so they can drift off to sleep.

CHAPTER TWO

I'll Take Household Chores for 800, Alex (A *Jeopardy* Category Nobody Wins)

When I was little, I used to play house. I would be the wife and I would pretend to serve delicious hot, homemade meals to my husband. I would effortlessly take care of our well-behaved babies. Now that I am the wife and mom, I find that playing house is exhausting. Homemade meals are a joke and require time that I simply don't have. Everyone leaves their shit all over the place, and I need some damn help with the effing chores. Playing house can lead to a lot of arguments, so get ready to "dish" on the dishes.

DISHWASHERS ARE FOR SANITIZING PURPOSES ONLY

I wash every dish before it goes into the dishwasher. I mean wash, like *really* wash. I use soap, water, the whole nine yards. I scrub, rinse, repeat. Then I load the dishwasher in the proper format. Cups on the outside upper rack, bowls in the proper place on the bottom rack, followed by plates, Tupperware, and silverware. The silverware should of course be sorted by forks, knives, and spoons so that when you are unloading, it is already organized and ready to go into the drawer.

When the dishwasher is full, I run it in order to sanitize the dishes. I want that hot soapy water to kill any and all bacteria, so that I can eat off these plates and forks knowing that I will not die of salmonella poisoning. It is pretty simple.

My husband, on the other hand, believes that the dishwasher is actually going to wash the dishes for him. He puts them in dirty. He puts them in the wrong spot. (See correct placement above.) He ignores all of the dishwasher etiquette rules for loading and sorting. He does not use soap. It is utter chaos.

Most earth-shattering of all, he always puts the bowls in with pieces of Fruity Pebbles still stuck on. I know that he does this because, for whatever misguided reason, he fully believes that the dishwasher is going to clean old, dried food off the dishes, but that is just plain stupid. I have never owned a dishwasher that actually cleaned a cereal bowl that was loaded with cereal still stuck on it. Like *never*. Not once in my life have I unloaded a bowl that was put in with Raisin Bran on it and have it come out clean. Now maybe that's because I can't afford a top-notch dishwasher, but I don't think so. I think it's because, like I have said a million times, my husband is wrong and a dishwasher's sole purpose is for sanitizing.

Every time I ask my husband to wash the dishes, we have the same conversation.

ME: (*opening dishwasher*) For. The. Love. Dave, can you please come here?

HUSBAND: What?

ME: I asked you to wash the dishes.

HUSBAND: I did.

ME: No, you put the dirty dishes into the dishwasher and put them in the wrong spot.

HUSBAND: You can hear yourself talking, right? There isn't a right or wrong way to load a dishwasher.

ME: You must like eating off dirty dishes, because you didn't wash any of these.

HUSBAND: YOU GET THAT I PUT THEM IN THE DISHWASHER, RIGHT? LIKE, THAT IS THE DISHWASHER'S JOB.

ME: THE DISHWASHER IS FOR SANITIZING PURPOSES ONLY! FUCK!

HUSBAND: You're fucking nuts.

ME: You're going to give this entire family flesh-eating bacteria.

HUSBAND: No I'm not. You're going to rewash them anyway.

ME: GO AWAY!

And yet I continue to ask him to do the dishes, even though I know what is going to happen. He will do the dishes and then I will go back and rewash the dishes and load them in the proper sequence. I know that this makes me look crazy, but I don't care. In my heart of hearts, I know that there is a proper way to do this: my way. I might not be able to get him to load the dishwasher on my terms, but I will die trying.

THE KEEPER OF ALL THINGS

In my home, I am the keeper of all things. I mean EVERYTHING. I am the one who is supposed to know where every sock, every roll of toilet paper, and every piece of important "red envelope" urgent mail is kept. I am also tasked with keeping the family calendar. I need to remember what day my son's soccer game is, what time gymnastics practice pickup is, and For. The. Love. I can never remember to pack school lunches the night before. I guess I am tasked with this because I am the wife and mother, but I am truly not responsible enough for this. Over the years, I have forgotten to put pants on before leaving the house. (That makes for an awkward school drop-off line situation when the crossing guard asks you to roll down the window.)

One time I even forgot to pick up my son from school. I got busy doing a million things and I totally forgot. I know what you are thinking: that is the opposite of what Susan would do. You would be correct—I am pretty much the opposite of

Susan in every way. I thought I was going to die when I got a phone call from the school.

School Receptionist: Hello, Mrs. Masony?

Me: Yes, hi. This is Mrs. Masony.

School Receptionist: Were you planning on picking up Matias today?

Me: Of course I am. I am on my way right now. (*I was totally lying. I was not on my way.*)

School Receptionist: Wonderful. He has been sitting in the office for 35 minutes.

Me: I am so sorry. I am on my way.

(This is the actual note that was left for me at the front desk the day I forgot to pick up my son from school. I took a picture of the note because I knew at some point in the future I would be able to laugh at this. The day it happened, however, I didn't laugh. I felt hot and sweaty. I felt like the eyes of every mom on the planet were looking at me and judging me. I thought about the awful things Susan would think and say about me. Luckily, I no longer care what Susan thinks.)

On top of my own inability to stay organized and responsible, I have three kids and a husband who lose everything. Like, everything they own. It amazes me that they don't walk out the door naked with just one sock on each day. I mean, it truly amazes me.

I get that when my son was a seven-year-old he needed help with his shoes in the morning, but why do I have to help my husband locate his shoes? He is a 41-year-old, highly intelligent, logical thinker, and for the most part, a responsible adult. Why is it that he can't keep track of his shoes, wallet, watch, or clothing, for that matter? I can't tell you how many times we have had to cancel credit cards because my husband lost his wallet. Honestly, it is embarrassing. Best part, we usually find it a few days later after the cards have been canceled and new ones are in the mail. I have found his wallet under the bed, under the couch, under the front seat of my minivan, in the dog crate, behind the toilet, and one time in a kitchen cabinet. I bet if I called the credit card company, they could tell me how many new cards have had to be issued for his account. I bet that I was also noted on the account as the "crazy woman who was screaming in the background cursing husband's existence and inability to his keep wallet safe."

I'm sure in some way, shape, or form, this is my fault. Let's be honest: everything is always my fault. Lost shoes, lost wallets, lost sanity—it usually gets traced back to me. It comes with the job of being The Keeper of All Things. However, being The Keeper of All Things is unrealistic and unattainable. No one can do it all, be it all, take care of it all. We slip. We fail. We forget our kids at school pickup. I know someone is reading this and thinking she will absolutely, without a doubt, never forget to pick up her kid from an activity, but NEVER SAY NEVER—that shit will most likely happen. We learn from it, and thank God, we move on. I urge you to find the ability to move on. It will make life easier, and saying, "Oh fuck it" is actually pretty freeing.

THAT'S NOT DIRTY!

When I am not keeping track of everyone's everything, I am usually doing dishes, laundry, cooking, or some combination of those tasks. I don't know about you, but I actually don't hate household chores. The problem is that they become super monotonous. I think laundry is the one that kicks me in the ass the most.

Let me be crystal clear. I am the only person in the house who does laundry. I do all of the washing and folding. My kids and my husband do not help me. My husband will only do laundry if I am out of town for over three consecutive days, because they end up running out of clean underwear. He will wash the laundry and dry it, but then it gets thrown on the couch, and everyone picks out what they need. My husband doesn't think laundry needs to be folded. He believes that it could just be shoved in dresser drawers, like we are a bunch of filthy animals.

My husband calls me the laundry thief. I literally walk around all day picking up clothing from the floor, the couch, the kitchen counters, you name it. I have found underwear hanging off ceiling fans. I constantly see islands of clothes that make it look like my family members evaporated—POOF—and all that is left behind is a pile of socks, pants, a shirt, and sharty underpants.

Almost every single day my husband and I argue over the laundry. He will leave a shirt or a pair of shorts on the floor and I will pick them up and put them in the laundry. Later on in the day, he will go and look for said floor shorts or shirt and yell, "Where are my shorts? I left them right here." I will scream back, "You left them on the floor, so they were dirty. I picked them up and put them in the wash." He will then passionately shout back, "THEY WERE NOT DIRTY! STOP TAKING MY CLOTHING!" I will then lovingly yell, "THEN STOP LEAVING IT ON THE FLOOR! FOR THE LOVE OF ALL THINGS HOLY!!!"

This romantic dance has gone on every day for years. I am not exaggerating. EVERY. SINGLE. DAY. In my mind, if a piece of clothing is on the floor, it is dirty. Why should I assume that anyone would put clean clothing on the floor? It truly makes no sense to me. I also can't stand the fact that he gets irritated that I took the clothing. I am the one who picked it up and washed the damn thing, and he has the nerve to get mad at me??? Really??? Like, get the hell outta here, you have lost your damn mind! How hard is it to take the item you were wearing and fold it up and put it on your pillow? Or just fold it and put it away if it isn't dirty? How does he not get that putting something on the floor equals dirty? The man is a math whiz, he has taken transcendental calculus, yet he wants to argue with me over floor shorts? It is a very simple if/then mathematical statement: If clothing is on the floor, then said clothing is dirty.

Done. Period. Simple. I wonder if this is why animals don't wear clothing?

THIS IS HOW YOU FOLD A TOWEL IF YOU WANT TO GET DIVORCED

I know, I know, I am legit crazy. I get it. I can hear the words as they come out of my mouth, but I do believe that there is a right and a wrong way to fold laundry. I also know that when I ask my husband to help me with the laundry, he will not do it my way. I know that I should be happy that he is helping and I should accept his help, but I don't. I get pissed every time he folds a towel wrong and I have to refold it.

In my house, we have a shelf that the towels go on. We are short on storage in our bathroom. In order for the towels to fit on the shelf they have to be folded in half once, then a second, a third, and roll, roll, roll:

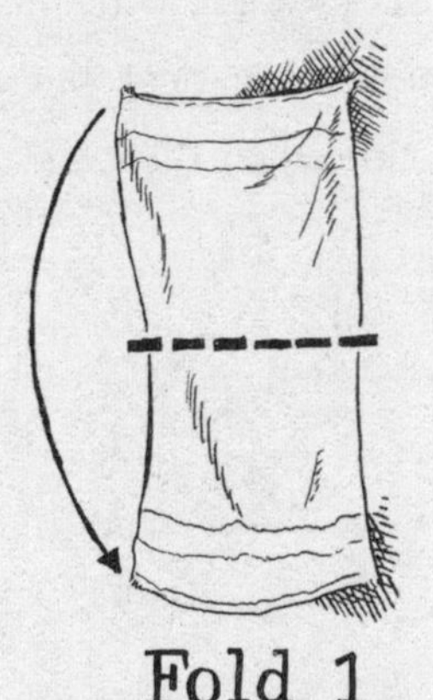

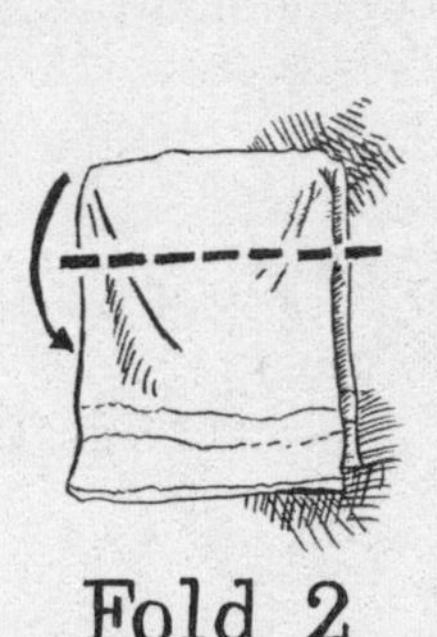

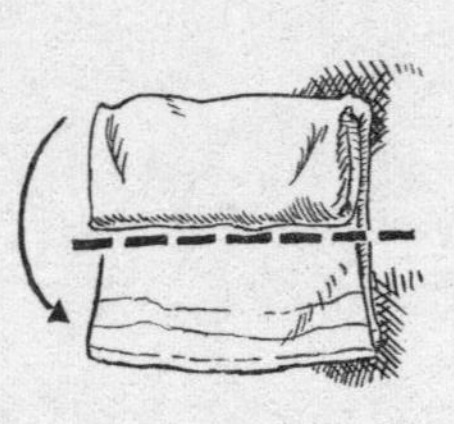

It is pretty simple. I only have so much shelf space, and so many towels, so they need to be folded in this manner to all fit. I have shown my husband how several times, given adequate tutorials, and yet each time he folds them like this:

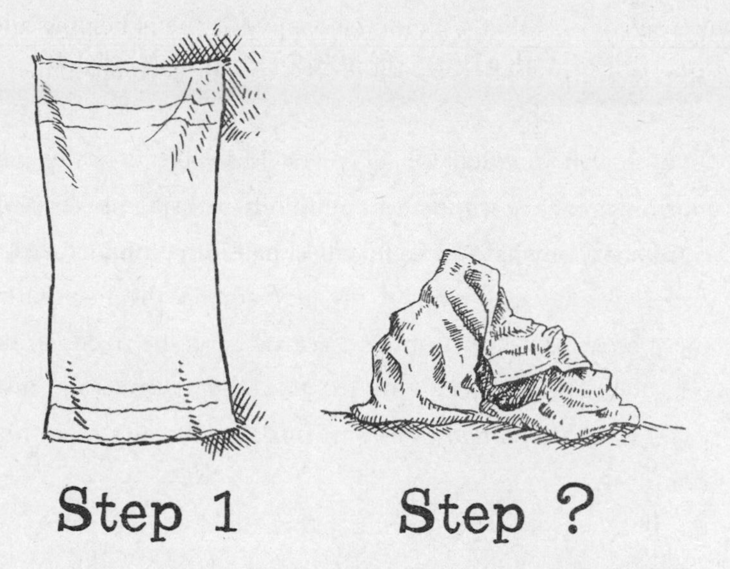

When I see this display of inadequately folded laundry, I look at him and say, "It's like you want to get divorced." I know it's crazy, but in that moment, I am positive his inability to fold the towels properly is his way of saying, "I asked for a blow job last week and didn't get one, so I am going to improperly fold this towel to piss you off." I mean, in what universe does this not make your skin crawl? I know that my husband does not have an intimate connection to the laundry like I do, but when I ask him to fold the damn towel so it will properly fit on the damn shelf, I really want him to PROPERLY ROLL AND FOLD THE DAMN TOWEL! Anyone have any questions on how to properly fold the towels? (I know my husband is reading this and raising his hand.)

CONGRATULATIONS ON DOING THE BARE MINIMUM!

I have been married for 17 years. Marriage is really hard work. Yes, I said *work*. Sustaining our marriage takes dedication, willingness to compromise, passion, empathy, desire, and self-control to not hit my husband in the face with a piece of two-by-four lumber. I am sure that he needs to rely on a ton of self-control with me as well. I am no walk in the park. If we are being honest, my husband doesn't even think I'm funny.

But, one Sunday after church, I decided to go to the gym. I normally don't leave the house in complete shambles, but I couldn't look at the mess any longer. I told my husband I'd be back in an hour and off I went. When I arrived home, I opened the door to my husband vacuuming the floors. It was a sight I don't normally see. In our house, I am the primary person who does the dishes, cleans the bathrooms, does the laundry, and pretty much takes care of all the domestic duties except cooking. My husband took over the cooking in 2018 and I fell in love with him all over again. Back to my story. I stepped into the house and my husband looked at me and said, "Look! I cleaned the house. Come, let me show you what I have done." He then proceeded to walk me through the house, showing me each and every task he had completed. He then said, "Do you love it or what?!?"

I am not sure which stunned me more, the fact that he was cleaning the house or that he was asking for accolades and praise for cleaning the house. I had been cleaning our home for the past 17 years and I've never walked him around the house to show him what I had done. Good Lord, if I did that, I wouldn't do anything but walk him around the house showing him all the shit I do on a daily basis. It did, however, make me wonder why men need to be praised for doing household chores. We both live here. However, the second he cleans a dish, he needs approval and praise. WTF?!?!?!?!?

I was happy he pitched in and cleaned up, but it made me a bit angry that he wanted to be praised and glorified for the things I do several times a day, each day of my life. Like, really, buddy? Seriously? If I took him by the hand every time I did the dishes, the laundry, picked up other people's shit and put it where it belonged, he would be attached to my hip all day. I don't do all of these tasks each and every day because I am waiting to be praised. I do them because they need to be done. I do them because I don't want to end up on an episode of *Hoarders*. I do them because I love my family. I agree that it is nice to be noticed and praised, but FOR THE LOVE, we all need to pitch in.

I made a video about this interaction with my husband and the internet gave me some interesting feedback on our situation. News flash! I was not the only wife to have this exact discussion with her husband.

Here are just a few of the comments:

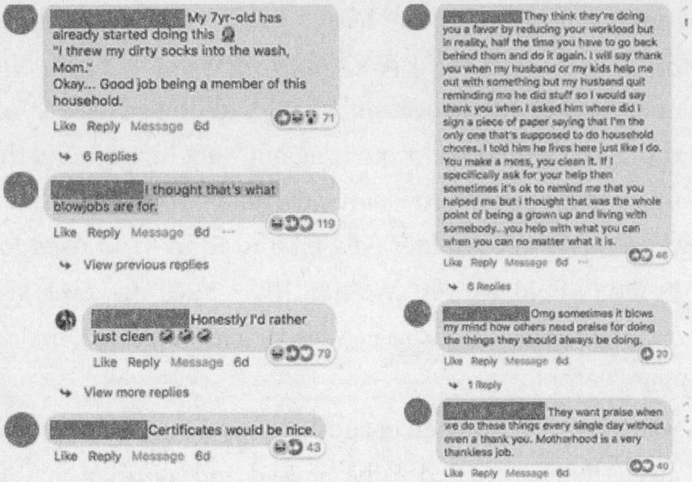

My 7yr-old has already started doing this 😩
"I threw my dirty socks into the wash, Mom."
Okay... Good job being a member of this household.
Like Reply Message 6d 71
6 Replies

I thought that's what blowjobs are for.
Like Reply Message 6d 119
View previous replies

Honestly I'd rather just clean
Like Reply Message 6d 79
View more replies

Certificates would be nice.
Like Reply Message 6d 43

They think they're doing you a favor by reducing your workload but in reality, half the time you have to go back behind them and do it again. I will say thank you when my husband or my kids help me out with something but my husband quit reminding me he did stuff so I would say thank you when I asked him where did I sign a piece of paper saying that I'm the only one that's supposed to do household chores. I told him he lives here just like I do. You make a mess, you clean it. If I specifically ask for your help then sometimes it's ok to remind me that you helped me but i thought that was the whole point of being a grown up and living with somebody...you help with what you can when you can no matter what it is.
Like Reply Message 6d 46
6 Replies

Omg sometimes it blows my mind how others need praise for doing the things they should always be doing.
Like Reply Message 6d 20
1 Reply

They want praise when we do these things every single day without even a thank you. Motherhood is a very thankless job.
Like Reply Message 6d 40

It's mind blowing. I am in fact not the only one dealing with this. I know that men and women are wired differently, but when things need to be done, everyone should pitch in to get them done. I hope that someday, in the near future, my husband looks into the sink and sees the dishes and thinks, "These are dirty. They need to be washed. I shall wash them. I will wash them because I am a part of this household and I am a mature grown adult who understands the value of a job well done. I know that it is the right thing to do. I will not seek praise as a result of washing the dishes. I will simply do them and then go about my day. I will also NOT ask for a blow job as a reward for doing the dishes."

WHEN YOUR HUSBAND SAYS, "I COULDN'T CLEAN—THE KIDS WERE BAD."

In 2018, my husband took over the cooking and grocery shopping duties in our home. It was amazing and I am truly grateful that he decided to jump in, 15 years after we married, to participate in running the household. I'm kidding . . . I'm kidding. Side note: I do not think I am lucky that he does these things. He should be helping and so should your husband. He eats the food we purchase, so why shouldn't he be involved in the process?

So back to the point of this story. My husband is a very intelligent man. He is logical. He takes his time to figure things out and always devises a plan when starting a project. He is a perfectionist, which is pretty annoying, as I'm positive everything can be fixed with duct tape and Gorilla glue. So my very smart, very logical husband makes a list and goes to the grocery store each week. However, every time he goes to the grocery store he calls or texts me to ask questions about the items, and asks me to check the fridge for various items. After all of that, he usually ends up coming home with at least two or three items that are wrong. What do I mean by wrong? He will come home with unsweetened soy milk instead of vanilla soy milk. He will come home with fat-free ice cream instead of the full-fat ice cream that I was dreaming about all day long.

Once again, someone reading this is going to say, "Bitch, please! Be happy he is going to the grocery store at all!" To you I say, why? I went to the grocery store for the first 15 years of our marriage and I didn't have to call him to double-check everything. Let me reiterate that he is a very smart man, so why can't he remember that I want full-fat ice cream? Unless he is trying to tell me something about my full-fat ice cream intake, in which case he needs to evaluate how much he likes breathing oxygen.

I just think it's time that we get our men to be actively involved in the mechanics of running a home. They need to know how hard it is to "take care" of the house so they can truly appreciate all that we do, day in and day out. When I started traveling for our business, my husband got a firsthand look at everything I do each day. The kids, the dishes, the laundry, the cooking, the cleaning, the shit that is required to make it all happen. The first several trips I took, I would come home to a massive mess. The house would look like a bomb exploded. Dishes would be in the sink. Floors sticky, no laundry would be done. Just a massive mess.

One time after I came home from a three-day trip, I lost it. I walked in and the house was in complete disarray. Dishes were piled up in the sink. The laundry pile resembled Mount Everest and there were toys all over the house. When I asked my husband why the house was so messy, he said, "I couldn't clean up—the kids were bad." I wasn't exactly sure what that meant, because I also live with those same kids, and they are bad when they are home with me, and yet I somehow manage to clean the house.

I sat down in the massive pile of laundry and I just snapped. Here is our exchange as I remember it.

ME: Why couldn't you do the laundry? There are four days' worth of laundry here and it smells awful!

HUSBAND: I didn't want to do the laundry.

ME: Isn't it enough that I want you to do the laundry?

HUSBAND: No one wants to do laundry!

ME: I know that, but we HAVE to do laundry. LOOK AT ALL THIS LAUNDRY!

HUSBAND:

ME: I WANT YOU TO WANT TO DO THE LAUNDRY!!!!!!!!

HUSBAND: (*He is now laughing.*) No one wants to do the laundry.

I wanted him to WANT to do the laundry because laundry is a priority in my mind. I do laundry each and every day. The washer and dryer are always going at my house. If I stay on top of the laundry, I feel like I have accomplished something. When I go out of town and all of the laundry piles up, I feel immediately defeated when I get home. Instead of saying that to him, I screamed, "I WANT YOU TO WANT TO DO THE LAUNDRY!"

Looking back on this argument, I can see where we went wrong. We both had communication issues and we both handled the situation poorly. I do try to state exactly what I need and want to see happen now. It doesn't always turn out that way, but we are working on it. Like I said earlier, marriage is a shit-ton of work. And my husband was right about one thing: no one wants to do the laundry, or the dishes, or the grocery shopping.

INSIDE THE BOWL. INSIDE THE HAMPER. ARE YOU EVER LISTENING TO ME?

This one might seem familiar to you. It's the middle of the night. You walk into the bathroom in the dark. You feel something wet on the floor. Your foot is now definitely touching urine. You are sure of it. You go to sit on the toilet and now your ass is wet. Not in a good kind of way, rather an "I'm definitely sitting on someone's urine" kind of way. You have repeatedly asked your husband to lift the seat when urinating, as well as to get it INSIDE THE BOWL; however, you are in a Groundhog Day scenario, and you let out a sigh. You realize this is your life and you will be asking him to piss in the bowl and lift the seat for the next 40 years, God willing.

In this instance, how am I supposed to not give instructions? How am I not supposed to repeatedly ask him to lift the seat and piss in the bowl? He says he is going to, but he never does. I guess I'm an optimist. I truly believe that at some point I will sit to pee and the seat will be urine free. I'm naïve and gullible, but I WANT to believe that he WANTS to piss INSIDE the bowl. I'm not sure how marriage and motherhood haven't beaten that out of me yet, but I really want to believe it.

How about another example of my family's constant need for basic direction. Do you ever walk around your house and find clothing on the floor? YOU DO? How did I know that? Well, I can't walk more than ten feet without finding someone's clothing on the floor. Socks, underwear, pants, clothing they only wore for about 2.5 nanoseconds. My kids are the worst offenders, but my husband plays a part by constantly putting clothes NEXT to the hamper. Not IN the hamper, but NEXT to the hamper. He also loves to put the clothes that he is going to "wear again" on the chair next to his bed. These are the clothes that I go to pick up to wash and he says, "Those aren't dirty." I will say, "Why are they here then, and not put away?" He always replies, "I am going to wear them again." In my mind, I am shouting, "When? When the fuck are you going to wear them again?" It's just a fun little game we play to keep our marriage spicy, and it reminds me to keep his life insurance plan up to date.

It is really hard not to "nag" your spouse or kids when they clearly do not do what is asked of them. "Please pick up your toys. Please put the dishes in the sink. Please put a damn trash bag in the damn trash can!" I ask over and over and over and over again. I get that they are kids and I get that no one really wants to clean up, but shit needs to get done. I repeat myself just in case they have forgotten. Perhaps they really didn't remember that the dirty dishes go in the sink. Perhaps they have chore-related amnesia. Perhaps they like the sound of my shrill voice screaming about the dishes and trash. Whatever the case, I have not found a solution to the nagging situation. I could stop asking people around the house to do things, but in less than a month we would be in a trash pile the size of Texas. So, if you were looking for advice on getting your spouse and kids to pick their own crap up, I'm not your gal. I'm the lady you can hear yelling at her kids when the windows are open.

CHAPTER THREE

Family Time:
WE NEED TO ENJOY EVERY FUCKING MINUTE, OR ELSE!

Family is tricky. Really, really tricky. We are told to love our family members unconditionally, but then they go and do something that is so stupid or awful that we want to disown them. Blood is thicker than water, but some of my relatives are super thick (dense, thick-headed, obtuse, and slow-witted), and that can be exhausting. Still, as I get older, I've realized that time is fleeting and it's important to spend time with our families, even those members who still think my husband is just a really tan "white guy." How on earth is that possible? I mean, you've heard him say grace in Spanish and you've met my in-laws, for crying out loud, Aunt Linda. He is not white! Go ahead and clutch your pearls while looking for your fainting chair.

14 Steps to an Epic Holiday-Palooza Party Because 15 Steps Might Kill a Bitch

1. Make sure to invite only the relatives that you enjoy spending time with. DO NOT INVITE SUSAN! I don't care if you text, send snail mail, or extend the invite over the phone.

2. Start to plan your event based on the number of RSVPs that you received. Wait three days. Realize that only half have replied, and then send out the reminder text so that they can ignore those instructions as well.

3. Get a phone call from your mother or mother-in-law, reminding you that you "forgot" to invite a relative. You damn well know that you didn't forget anything, but now you will have to invite said relative and look like an ass while extending the late invitation.

4. Begin to prep for the epic holiday event by buying way too much food and paper goods. Use all the coupons you have been saving for toilet paper, napkins, and paper plates, and then think to yourself, "Freaking hell, I was so excited to get that toilet paper at a discount, and now every relative I know will be wiping their ass with my on-sale toilet paper."

5. Look at the calendar and realize you are a week out from the epic holiday extravaganza and you are still missing several RSVPs and also received two more phone calls from your mother or mother-in-law, stating that there are a few last-minute guests she would like you to invite. When you ask why she can't extend the invitation, she tells you that it would come best from you. Of course, it would, DUH!

6. Start to panic as the event is in three days and you forgot to order the pies. It's fine; you can get some at the store. DON'T PANIC. You stop at the store and get the pies. Your mother-in-law comes by the house to do an inspection—I mean, comes for a visit—and she sees the pecan pie. She begins to scream at you because your cousin's mother's husband is allergic to nuts and how could you be so thoughtless??? You now need more pie.

7. Cry.

8. Begin to clean the house two days before, and throw out, organize, and rearrange everything you own. Vacuum, mop, dust. (Realize you haven't dusted in at least six months. It looks like it is snowing in the house.) Round one of cleaning has been accomplished.

9. The kids come home from school and ruin everything you just did.

10. Cry.

11. It's now the day of the wonderful, epic holidaypalooza. You start round two of cleaning by doing laundry, washing dishes, hiding toys, and whisper-screaming about how you should have never hosted this godforsaken event.

12. Open the wine.

13. Cook. Cook like you know what the hell you are doing. Well, properly heat the food at least. I am no cook, so I usually thaw, heat, and claim it as my own. It's amazing how tasty a frozen store-bought casserole can be. If that isn't good enough for you, Cousin Steve, well, you can suck it.

14. Doorbell rings and the epic holiday-palooza begins!!! You are now on the clock to make this event magical and full of memories. Crack open that second bottle of wine, because your mother-in-law's passive-aggressive comments about your canned green bean casserole are coming in hot and you are sporting a perma-cringe smile for the next four to six hours. You can do this!!!

IT'S A FAMILY TRIP, NOT A VACATION: FIVE WAYS TO TELL THE DIFFERENCE

I love my children, but if we are traveling with them, it's not a vacation, it's a trip. There is a big difference between a vacation and a trip. If you are unaware of the differences, ask yourself the following questions to identify whether you're on a vacation or a trip:

1. Is the hotel you are staying at themed with cartoon characters or animals, or located at a theme park? If you answered yes, and your kids are still with you, you are on a family trip. If you answered yes and the kids are not with you, why the fuck are you at a cartooned-themed hotel? Leave immediately and find a spa that serves umbrella drinks.

2. Have you recently given someone other than yourself a snack or drink? Have you wiped a butt other than your own? If you said yes, I think you know where this is going . . . this is a family trip. If you answered no, I am totally jealous and you are definitely on vacation.

3. Did you sleep in past 8 A.M. and wake up in a dry bed, free of urine? Just look over to your right or left—is there a tiny foot in your face? See where I am going with this? If you answered no to the first question and yes to the second, you are on a family trip. If you see no tiny feet and you are urine free, way to go—this is an epic vacation.

4. Have you had to stop what you are doing because a level-seven temper tantrum erupted in a gift shop, due to you not purchasing your child an overpriced key chain that says "Susan" on it, rather than your child's name, "Lilly"? You, my poor friend, are on a family trip. If you answered no, I am so impressed that you are on vacation right now. You might be in a gift shop, but you are there buying gifts for the children that you left at home, which means no one you own is throwing a fit by the stuffed animal section.

5. Once again, please take a look at your surroundings. Are your children anywhere near you? If you answered yes, then you are in fact on a family trip. If you answered no, make sure they aren't lost, and that you actually left them with a sitter, because you, my friend, are on a vacation.

Don't get me wrong—family trips can be fantastic, but they are a ton of work. You are still the primary caregiver. You are still feeding kids, taking them to the bathroom, and stopping what you are doing so you don't miss a nap that will ensure there isn't a volcanic eruption at the Disney-themed restaurant that you grossly overpaid for. You are making memories, but you are also still yelling at your children to stop touching the public restroom toilet seats. It is not relaxing for the parents.

Vacations, on the other hand, are relaxing. You are only worrying about you and that fine dad bod you have sitting across from you. You have drinks with umbrellas in them and breakfast that does not include Mickey Mouse pancakes. You can have sex. You can take a nap. You can poop in peace. There are so many options for your time. And the silence—don't get me started on how *quiet* quiet is! It is, like, so freaking quiet. Time to unwind and enjoy; you deserve this. Make those memories and take that nap!

PICK YOUR BATTLES: HOW TO PROPERLY FIGHT WITH YOUR IN-LAWS

Technically, you picked your in-laws when you married your spouse. I know that seems like a bit of a stretch, but if you agreed to marry that person after meeting his/her crazy family, that is on you. Most families are crazy, even though people deny it, or don't post about it on social media. My family is crazy and so is my husband's. They are also full of love, even when that love is misguided and crosses boundaries. So, once you are married and his/her family is your family, what do you do when you get into a fight?

I have had many, many fights with my in-laws. At one point, we were estranged for almost ten months. I had no contact with them; I even blocked them from my phone. My husband still spoke to them, and we never kept the children from them, but it was necessary for me to step out of the picture for my own sanity. I decided after discussing things with my husband that we needed to try to save the relationship. We set boundaries for the meeting. We refused to rehash the argument that took place ten months earlier. We set rules moving forward. During the initial argument, I said things I shouldn't have said, and my in-laws said things they shouldn't have said. After the family meeting, my mother-in-law sent me a card stating she was sorry that I acted in such a way that she needed to treat me the way she did. Even in her "apology" she blamed me for the argument.

So, when it comes to fighting with in-laws, I have been through it. I do have some advice on picking your battles with your in-laws, as well as on how to fight fair. Here are 11 tips, because clearly ten isn't enough.

1. Never hang up on your MIL, even if what she said was completely rude and hurtful. Strike that: she most likely wanted to be rude and hurtful, but you don't have to join the bitchy brigade. Walk tall, my friend, even though that is really, REALLY hard to do.

2. Don't call your MIL a crazy-ass bitch. You might feel better the second you say it, but you will eventually feel worse. She may very well be a crazy-ass bitch, but saying it actually says more about you and less about her. Do I know this from firsthand experience? you ask. Ummmmm, maybe.

3. Don't fight over things that won't matter tomorrow. The small stuff, like the in-laws feeding your kids too much chocolate or soda. This won't be an issue forever. However, if the kids have specific dietary issues or allergies, they need to follow those rules. Those rules are for safety and health, and that's not you overreacting.

4. If your MIL is a shopper and she is always buying things for your kids, and you have repeatedly asked her to stop, and she refuses to, try what I did. Every time she would buy multiple items for my kids that they didn't need (stuffed animals, toys, clothing), I would donate them. Once the kids told her that I was donating them, she stopped buying them. We were helping out other families by donating, and eventually she realized that I really didn't want more stuff in my house. I didn't even have to have an altercation with her.

5. It also used to bother me that she would buy my kids shoes at the beginning of the school year. I felt like she was making a statement that I couldn't buy shoes for my own children. I realized that was silly. Why was I fighting with someone who was going to provide shoes for my kids, no matter what her motive was? My kids needed new shoes and I didn't have to buy them. It was a win. I really don't care what her motive was. I am going to assume her motive was pure and buying shoes for my kids brought her joy.

6. If you invite your in-laws to family events and they refuse to come or they come and make things uncomfortable, stop inviting them. Once they have made it clear that they don't want to come, you don't need to extend the gesture. If they change their minds, they are adults, who have phones; they can call you and inquire about events. Don't put yourself in a situation where you are always pissed off about them not showing up, or pissed that they came and ruined something. You get to choose who you spend time with. YOU ARE AN ADULT. I know our parents and in-laws can make us feel like children, well into our

40s and 50s, but hey, you wear big-girl undies, so act like it. I know, I know. This is so much easier said than done. I feel you. I so do.

7. Be honest, but do your absolute best to not be hurtful when you're communicating with your in-laws. It never helps anyone to call names or send nasty text messages. I know that those types of responses come from a place of hurt, but they only continue to perpetuate a cycle of hurt. The last time I got into a massive blowout with my in-laws, I blocked my MIL's phone number. It was really easy to not send nasty text messages when she couldn't text me in the first place.

8. Set very specific boundaries around how you will speak to each other, spend time with each other, and spend time with the kids. If your in-laws say something that upsets you, calmly explain that to them. They may not know they hurt your feelings. Most of the time people are hurt by the tone of the words, rather than the words themselves. So be specific when you explain why you are feeling the way you are feeling. I am super guilty of this. My tone and my face speak volumes. I have to try to remember that when I am conversing with my in-laws. My words are saying, "Please don't give the kids ice cream." My face is saying, "Seriously! SON OF A BITCH! PLEASE! NO MORE FUCKING ICE CREAM. They have diarrhea for days after ice cream. I don't care how much they love it and love you for it. I pay the ultimate price later, as they shit their brains out in an apocalyptic bathroom battle that ends with tears and things that cannot be unseen."

9. If you need a break from your in-laws, take it. Sanity is a rare commodity these days. We are overscheduled, overworked, and overwhelmed. I totally understand that in-laws are family, but when the relationship gets toxic, you have to cut the toxic people out of your life. It doesn't need to be a forever thing, but creating distance can help defuse the situation and bring you some much-needed peace. Life is stressful enough without the people who created the love of your life telling you how disappointed they are that you can't make a proper meal suited for their son. Guess what, mommy dearest, your son has a pair of fucking arms and can read a cookbook. He's got this.

10. You cannot change your in-laws. They are who they are. They will do things that piss you off and at times they will create and cause utter chaos in your life. The only thing you can do is choose whether to be involved in the chaos. My MIL truly believes that the infamous argument of 2017 was all my fault. I can't change that. All I can do is control my own emotions and actions. This is not easy, but it is so important to that whole sanity thing I was talking about before.

11. Life is simply too short, so don't live an unhappy life. I used to think that if my in-laws moved, it would create some space and I would find more peace. My MIL knows how to cause chaos from hundreds of miles away, just by making a phone call. I have decided that I have to let things go. I can't harbor the hurt feelings or resentments for things said. My life, my kids' lives, and my marriage deserve better. So, I do my very best to let things go and only worry about the person in the equation who I can control: myself.

As you are reading this you might be thinking, easier said than done. I feel you. I know. I promise. None of it is easy, but after 17 years of marriage and dealing with in-laws, I've learned that this is the best way to find your sanity and know that you did your best with the relationship. Having awful in-laws is as exciting as the prospect of getting herpes, but we have to find a way to coexist. Just sayin'.

TOO MUCH QUALITY TIME IS A REAL THING

I have three delightful blessings. I love spending time with them, but winter break 2018 broke me. My kids were off from school for 23 days straight. *Twenty-three days.* We ate every meal together. We spent almost every single second together. The youngest even slept in our bed for the entire break. I don't think I like anyone enough to spend 23 days straight with them.

Eventually you look at your children and think, "Gosh, you really did inherit all of my awful qualities." I know you are probably gasping and thinking, what an awful thing to say about your children, but honestly, I don't care. That was my honest response after 23 days together. It was the first winter break that my husband spent with us in its entirety. The tension in our home was as thick as the Strategic Arms Limitation Talks between the US and Russia during the Cold War. I'm pretty sure he is still scarred from it. The kids fought nonstop. We had the holiday stress weighing on us. It was just the perfect storm of emotions, chaos, and family issues, and to top it off, my husband had a knee surgery that went sideways. Like super sideways. He ended up in the hospital with double-lung pneumonia and was under a doctor's care for a possible blood clot. All of this was swirling around while my kids were fighting about what episode of Dude Perfect to watch, and begging for a list of Christmas items that would make Prince George and Princess Charlotte of Cambridge blush.

It made me realize that time apart is truly necessary to remain sane. It also made it abundantly clear that my kids need to be separated in order for my husband and me to give each one of them the proper amount of attention. We took all three kids out together each time we had an outing. We NEVER should have done that. They needed and wanted some time apart, and because we didn't have anyone to babysit, we did what we had to do. In hindsight, we should have each taken turns with the kids and done some things together and some things separately. Instead of us all going bowling, my husband could have taken the boys and I could have gone to Target with my daughter. We didn't really understand that they NEEDED time apart.

Siblings fight. I still fight with my 41-, 28-, and 26-year-old siblings. My kids fight all the time. I used to think it wasn't normal, but it really is. I thought the fighting was bad when they were eight, five, and four, but that was nothing compared to now. At the ages of 14, 11, and 10, they fight nonstop about EVERYTHING. Getting a 23-day dose of that kind of fighting gave me a reality check on the way I was parenting. Moving forward, we scheduled every break with activities and separated the kids as much as possible. I'm not saying that you shouldn't do things together as a family, I'm just saying you've got to know your limits. We all have limits . . . even our kids.

NO, YOU'RE HOSTING THANKSGIVING THIS YEAR!

When I was first married, I was so excited to host Thanksgiving. I wanted everything to be perfect. The house was spotless, the meal was edible, and I felt like I was an unstoppable force. Fast-forward 16 years, and it is safe to say I will not fight with anyone to host a holiday. Aunt Gracie wants to host? AWESOME. Thanksgiving at Uncle Eric's this year? YASSSS, PLEASE! Fourth of July at Aunt Diana's? RSVP me for a party of five! I love holidays; I simply do not want to host them anymore.

My house is rarely clean. I do not want to clean my house to host people who don't live in my house. Why on earth should other people get to eat a beautiful meal on a clutter-free kitchen table, or sit on a sofa that is free of clothing or dog hair? If I live in a disheveled home, why should these other people get to enjoy a clean home? I don't ever get to enjoy a clean home.

Furthermore, hosting a holiday always leads to a massive expense. A friend of mine told me about a woman she knew who sent invitations to her family for Christmas dinner. On the invitation, she stated that it was $25 per head for the meal. THAT LADY GOT IT RIGHT! Think about it. Do you really want to go to Walmart and spend $500 on food for one meal? I don't. I get that might sound callous, but I'm just being honest. If I got invited and there was a price, I would totally pay it. Think about it. We pay to eat out at restaurants. We pay for the ambiance. We pay for the drinks. We pay for the expensive meal because we don't have to prepare it or clean it up. Sign me up for some honey-glazed "tofu-ham-furky" and all the fixings.

Why do I want to cook a meal and do all the cleanup? I do that every day. I surely don't want to do that on a holiday. If we are being honest, how about we all go out to eat if possible and no one has to cook or clean? Like, seriously. Think about it. We cook and clean up almost every single day of our lives. When the fuck do we get a day off? *Holiday* implies a day off. I do not want to cook, clean, or entertain others on a holiday.

Inviting people into your home gives them the opportunity to comment on your home. That might seem like an odd thing to say, but I will never forget the time we had a Halloween party in 2005. Let me elaborate. My husband is from St. Croix, one of the Virgin Islands. Our home was decorated in a very tropical theme. One wall was orange, one was red, one was light blue. It was a disaster that only Hilary Farr and David Visentin from *Love It or List It* could have successfully tackled. The simple truth was that we were 25 years old, with no interior decorating experience that wasn't dorm-life related. This woman came up to me and said, "I can't believe you painted your wall for Halloween! I mean, that is dedication. No one would really ever paint their wall this color otherwise." I'm sorry, what? Yup, she actually said that. People are cray. Looking back, was it a poor decorating choice? Yes. However, who the fuck paints a wall for Halloween? She knew she was being shady.

Back to the whole cleaning thing. When you host a holiday, you have to clean before, clean during, and then clean after. It takes so much work to make your house look like you don't live there. Logically you shouldn't clean up before people come, because a mess will ensue, but I can't have people over the way we live. I have pulled underwear off tables, the floor, ceiling fans, you name it. Also, my guest bathroom, which is my kids' bathroom, always smells like urine. I need to scrub the tile before anyone can use that bathroom, or it basically smells like a high-traffic 7-Eleven restroom.

I am not a good cook. I burn everything. I refuse to follow a recipe. I am a disaster in the kitchen. I almost feel like it is rude to invite people over for a meal that I am cooking. Kind of like a cruel joke. I have good intentions, but nothing ever comes out the way I planned, which isn't shocking, as I am a poor planner. I rarely have all of the ingredients I need for a recipe, and I failed college algebra, so fractions are ROUGH! How many tablespoons are in two cups of butter? I have no fucking idea. And guess what—I am out of butter.

If you still aren't sold on never hosting a family holiday again, can I interest you in catering? I know what you are thinking: "That sounds super expensive." Well, guess what—it isn't. You can go to your local grocery store and have the damn deli do it. Have sandwich platters and prepared side dishes. In the end, celebrate the holiday, don't feed into the stress of preparing for and hosting the holiday. Just remember that the holiday and spending time with those important to you is the best part; don't feel pressured to construct the most magical holiday ever, at the expense of your sanity. Otherwise you might end up in the fetal position, crying about lumpy mashed potatoes and how ungrateful your cousin's new boyfriend is. Ain't nobody got time for that.

THE EPIC FAMILY ROAD TRIP OF 2019

In March of 2019, my husband came to me and said he had an amazing idea. He told me that he wanted to pack up our trusty minivan "Rhonda" and he wanted to drive to Salt Lake City, Utah, and back, covering over 6,500 miles in 21 days. Yes, my husband's brilliant idea was to take our family of five on an epic road trip, so that we could make memories that would last a lifetime.

I politely told him that he was fucking insane and that I would happily *fly* to Salt Lake City, Utah, and then fly home, once our trip was done. However, that was not an option. He told me that driving would offer us plenty of opportunities to spend time together, especially since our kids were growing up so fast, and this summer's vacation might be the last big trip we take, because our oldest would be going into high school in 2020.

My husband took the reins and started planning the epic family road trip. He spent a few months perfecting the itinerary. He planned all the stops and booked all the hotels. He bought road flares, bear spray, antivenom kits, first aid kits, and several other items that I would never, ever put into the classification of a "vacation" item.

We left southwest Florida on June 21. Three hours into our trip, just as we were approaching Orlando, our kids asked, "Are we there yet?" for the first time. That's right. One hundred twenty miles into a 6,500-mile trip, these assholes asked, "Are we there yet?" Well, children, do you see mountains? For fuck sake! That was the first time I saw my husband's eye twitch. It would twitch several hundred times more on the trip, but I will always remember the first twitch.

We drove for eight hours that day and made it to our first hotel. It was a Best Western Plus that was clearly a minus. When I opened the door to our room, the carpet was wet and it smelled like someone had set the furniture on fire. I went to the front desk to complain about the smoke smell and the receptionist told me that all of the rooms were non-smoking rooms. Apparently, the people who last stayed in the room didn't follow that policy, or they were cremating bodies; either way, I wasn't staying in that room. They moved us to the other side of the hotel. I was tired, the kids were tired, and I was unimpressed with my husband's failure to understand that I had a firm $150-a-night minimum price range for a hotel room. I guess he thought I was kidding.

We survived the night in the Best Western Minus and got back in the minivan. We made our way through Alabama, Mississippi, and Louisiana the next day. The epic family road trip was not a vacation. It was 24 hours a day of incarceration. Our epic family road trip was in fact a never-ending episode of *Locked Up*. If you've never seen it, *Locked Up* is a docuseries that goes to different prisons across the country and follows inmates to give you a taste of prison life. So yes, I am comparing my family vacation to prison life.

My son set up a commissary in the backseat of the minivan. He was selling Doritos to the other kids at a quarter a pop. He also had gum and juice boxes. My daughter started fashioning a shiv out of a Capri Sun straw, and the youngest became the snitch. I was quickly elevated to cell block bitch and my husband to the disgruntled warden.

My husband became obsessed with pulling into a gas station and setting a five-minute timer for restroom breaks. He would set his watch and then scream at us like we were a trained team of Navy SEALs who were propelling out of a helicopter on a midnight mission in Peru. On one such stop I took the kids into the bathroom, but there was only one bathroom in this gas station, and the person who was in it clearly ate some bad gas-station sushi. He was tearing it up in there. Finally, he got out and my kid started using one of the most unholy thrones I have ever seen. By the time it was my turn, I saw my husband screaming at the pump, pointing at his watch, and demanding that we get back in the car.

We'd made it about 30 minutes down the road when I told my husband that I had to pee. He looked at me and said, "You are going to have to hold it." I said, "I'm sorry, what? I've had three children. If you don't find me another gas station, I will never hold anything ever again, if you know what I mean." He pulled up the map on his phone and said there wasn't a gas station for 25 miles. At that point I made an executive decision to pull over and pee on the side of the road. I pulled into the first dirt road that I saw and ran around the minivan. I pulled down my pants and squatted. I made sure to check that I couldn't see the cars passing by on the road; that way I knew they couldn't see me. The problem was, I didn't turn my head in the other direction, and every car that was heading north had a direct view of my anus. And if that wasn't bad enough, the dirt road I had pulled into was a driveway. Just as I was finishing, a woman yelled, "Hey! What are you doing over there?" I shook off the tinkle and pulled up my pants and jumped into Rhonda like I was Cousin Bo from *The Dukes of Hazzard*, minus the hood-sliding antics.

We eventually made it to our first stop, the Grand Canyon. My husband thought it would be a great idea to take me to a giant death hole with our children, because I am afraid of heights. Don't get me wrong, it is an amazing sight to see; however, my anxiety was through the roof. I was positive one of the kids was going to trip over a rock and go tumbling down the side of the canyon to certain and imminent death. He then took it one step further and we hiked down into the canyon on a series of switchbacks that were being traveled by hundreds of people. I felt like I was in a waiting line for purgatory, where everyone was dressed like a tourist, all while screaming at my kids to stay inside of the mountain or face certain death. Once we got to the base of the ravine, my husband looked at me and the kids and said, "Isn't this breathtaking?" Yeah, it was fucking taking all the breath I had to keep everyone alive! He then spent the rest of the afternoon putting our kids on every rock and ledge to take pictures, and give me panic attacks. I love that man, but he is a sick son of a bitch.

We finally made it to Salt Lake City, Utah, on July 3. We met up with some friends of ours at our hotel swimming pool and ordered pizza. The kids played and I drank wine, trying to find those last shreds of sanity. The next day was the Fourth of July and we wanted to go to the parade in Park City. We woke up early and made our way up the mountain. Just as we started to drive up, the check engine light in Rhonda came on. No fucking way! I had just spent $2,500 fixing Rhonda before we left. She had only 100,000 miles on her, and she was a Honda, for crying out loud.

We white-knuckled it the rest of the way up the mountain, hit the parade, and then very slowly drove the minivan back to the hotel. We couldn't find a mechanic shop that was open, as it was a holiday. We spent the next two days at a Honda dealership, where they fixed some sensors in poor, broken-down Rhonda. Much like our family, Rhonda had been beaten down by the epic family road trip.

I ended up flying out of Salt Lake City to LA for a work trip, and my husband drove for four days straight, with the kids, all by himself. The epic family road trip covered 20 states and 6,500 miles. There were plenty of times that we all wanted to kill each other. However, to my husband's credit, we made some wonderful family memories. I can safely say that there will not be another epic family road trip anytime soon, but I will definitely take more trips with my family each year. We saw a ton of our amazing country and we get to keep these memories forever. Living a full life includes the good, the bad, and the ugly.

Side note: Rhonda made it home, but ended up dying a painful death in October of 2019. It was a truly sad day. I wanted to keep her and put her up on a block in the side yard, but it was time to let her go. She served us well. *Vaya con Dios*, Rhonda! You will be missed.

THANK YOU, TUMOR, YOU'RE THE BEST! A WAKE-UP CALL I WASN'T READY FOR . . . OR WAS I?

I had my first child in 2006. I was 25. I was in no way ready to be a mom. Looking back, I made so many mistakes. I was so hard on myself. I tried to control everything. Life quickly escalated.

We added baby number two in 2009 and then baby number three in 2010. At age 30, I had three kids under the age of five, two of whom were in diapers. Things were a bit chaotic between 2010 and 2014. I was working full time, running our home, and attempting to raise three kids, all while slowly resenting my husband more and more each day. Why was I resenting him? I was doing everything on my own. We both worked, but I was the one who did the housework, the drop-offs, and the pickups. I was the primary parent, cook, maid, laundress, and chauffeur. I thought being a good wife and mother meant that I had to do it all, be it all, and do it myself.

I had a terrible case of "Mommy Martyrdom." I became increasingly depressed. I logically knew I had a good life. I loved my husband. I loved and adored my three beautiful blessings. We had good jobs, but I was a shell of a person. I had no idea who I was anymore. My husband insisted that I get a hobby. That would make me feel better. I thought to myself, "I have hobbies: they include cleaning the house, doing endless laundry, scrubbing toilets, grocery shopping, and getting a steam facial when I unload the dishwasher or drain pasta on spaghetti night. I am a mom of three; when the fuck am I supposed to fit in a hobby?"

He was convinced that if I got out of the house I would feel better, and it was time to put some of my needs first. I couldn't agree more, but what on earth did I want to do with my time? I decided to start working out. I used to be a pretty good athlete. I'd hit the gym and get my life right. I started working out four times a week. I really enjoyed having some time to myself. I met some new friends at the classes I was taking at the gym. It was a great way to de-stress. A funny thing happened, however: I started feeling really sick. I have suffered from heartburn my entire life. I know that sounds dramatic, but from the time I was in middle school, I remember complaining that my heart hurt. I would have awful upset stomachs and a lot of pain in my chest. Looking back, it was acid reflux. By the time I was 18, I was taking over-the-counter reflux medication on a daily basis. My reflux medication wasn't helping at all anymore. No matter what I ate, I would get heartburn.

I made a doctor's appointment to discuss my awful heartburn. My primary care physician referred me to a gastroenterologist. I will never forget my first meeting with this doctor. I went in and started listing my complaints.

> Me: I have terrible heartburn. My throat hurts from the acid coming up. I can't eat anything without getting sick.
>
> Doctor: Look at you. You are in great shape. You're attractive. Let's adjust your medication and see how things go.
>
> Me: Uh, okay.

I left that appointment a bit confused. What did being thin and attractive have to do with being sick? Not only did that conversation make me uncomfortable, it made me feel crazy. Was I dreaming up these symptoms in my head? I went home and did what I was instructed to do. I took more medication.

Over the next few months my symptoms got worse. I was unable to keep food down. I had trouble swallowing, I had lost ten pounds and my hair was falling out, and most nights I had to sleep in a chair, because lying flat was impossible. I called the doctor's office and made another appointment.

> ME: I am still really sick. I've lost ten pounds. I am having trouble swallowing, and I have to sleep in a chair. This isn't normal. I would like a scope. I looked online and you can stick a camera down there to check things out, right?
>
> DOCTOR: Slow down. You look just fine. I could order a scope, but those are really expensive and it's probably not necessary.
>
> ME: I would really like a scope. I do not feel well.
>
> DOCTOR: Well, if your insurance covers it, we can schedule one.

This is the part where I am going to tell you to be an advocate for yourself. As moms, women, wives, we are constantly taking care of everyone else, and we forget to care for ourselves. We walk around wounded and sick and say, "I'm fine, it will be fine. I'm fine," when in fact we are not fine. I knew deep down in my core that I was not well.

I did my best to not overthink. I scheduled the endoscopy and did what everyone does, an online search of my symptoms on Google. *FUCK!!!!! I have cancer!* I knew it. I ran to my husband and said, "I just went online and searched my symptoms. I know I have esophageal cancer." "Stop," he said. "Just relax, and wait for the scan." A few weeks later, I was in the same-day surgery center being prepped for the best nap I had ever had in my life. Holy propofol! That is some serious shit. I felt like I slept for a week, and I was only out for about 20 minutes. We were ushered into a room with off-white walls and bad fluorescent lighting, an awful hotel-room picture hanging on the wall, and three lonely chairs. The doctor came in and said, "We found something. I'm not sure what it is, but we will have to send you to the hospital for an ultrasonic scope." *Something? He found something. What the fuck does that mean? I knew it. I freaking knew it.*

The next week was rough. I worried about my kids. I worried about my husband. I worried about who was going to do the laundry when I was dead. Apparently, I do care about the laundry. The next scope was just as much fun. I had a delightful propofol nap; however, when I woke up this time, I was looking at my husband.

ME: Hey.

HUSBAND: Hey.

ME: What did the doctor say? Where is he?

HUSBAND: He left. He told me that the something is a tumor.

ME: What? Are you serious? A tumor? Why did he leave?

HUSBAND: He said he can no longer treat you. He will call you later. He said you have to call an oncologist.

My poor husband had to deliver the news that I had a tumor in my esophagus. The look in his eyes when he said the word *tumor* made my heart break. I could see how scared he was.

At 34 years old, it was the first time I'd felt mortal. I'd never really thought about dying. I mean, I worried about car accidents and I watched way too much *Dateline* and *20/20* murder mysteries, but this was real. This was scary. This was a massive mind fuck. I spent the next few days trying to get in touch with an oncologist who could take my case. I cried a lot. I prayed a lot. I hid in my closet a lot. I was really concerned about my husband's future wife. That might sound weird, but I was worried about him finding someone to take care of him and the kids.

We chatted about my replacement. She would be a platinum blonde, perhaps an ex-gymnast. (That would be fun for him. I would be dead; it's cool if he has some fun.) She would need to have a nice set of tits and a firm behind. She would have to be a great cook, exceptional multitasker, and a very patient and caring mother. My replacement would be nothing like me. Talking about this actually made me laugh. I hadn't laughed in a while. I looked into my husband's eyes and began to cry.

Two weeks later, we were in the oncologist's office. The doctor was very matter-of-fact. He basically said he didn't know if I had cancer, but the tumor was crushing my esophagus. He didn't recommend a biopsy, due to the fact that if a piece of the tumor got into my bloodstream, and it was cancer, it would spread all over my body. He continued to explain that he would have to crack my chest and remove my esophagus to repair the damage.

ME: If it is cancer, what do we do?

DOCTOR: If it is esophageal cancer, you will have about a 5 percent survival rate. Once I get in there I will know what else needs to happen. You might wake up and we send you to hospice. You might wake up and be just fine. There is a range of things we need to consider. (*His words trailed off. My husband put his hand on my thigh and my mind snapped back to the conversation at hand.*)

ME: We're both teachers. School is getting ready to start. Can we wait until Thanksgiving break to do the surgery?

DOCTOR: If this is cancer, you might not have until Thanksgiving. You have four weeks to get your affairs in order.

FUCK. Well, good to know. "Affairs." My affairs? I apparently had to get my life right, and I had only four weeks to do it. *It's fine. I'm fine. It's going to be fine.* The next four weeks were a massive blur. I made freezer meals. I cleaned out my kids' rooms. I organized every bin and drawer in my house. I cleaned every surface, dusted fans, and scrubbed my tile grout with a toothbrush. If I was going to be dead soon, at least I would leave a clean house.

The night before my surgery, I lay in bed with my husband in silence. We were both thinking about the surgery, but neither of us said anything. I tried to be slick and I placed my hand on my husband's "business." I assumed sex would lighten the mood. I rolled over to kiss him and he was crying. I had never seen him cry. I mean, he got teary-eyed when the kids were born, but he was/is not an emotional man. We hugged and I told him to relax, everything was going to be fine. *I'm fine. It will be fine. Everything will be fine.*

The next morning, I was wheeled up to the operating room. I knew at that moment what the saying "crawling in your own skin" meant. I thought about pulling out my IV and running away. I asked my nurse for some medication to help me with my anxiety. She complied. She was a delight. I tried to convince the doctor to put breast implants in while he was "in there." He respectfully declined, as that was not his expertise. I then asked him to please not kill me, as I have three small children.

I woke up a few hours later to my handsome husband's face. I had tubes and wires coming out of everywhere. I couldn't talk, as I had a tube down my throat. I locked eyes with my husband and he said, "It's not cancer. You are going to be fine." I think I tried to tell him I loved him, but I passed back out. Eventually the doctor came in to check on me and explained the surgery. The tumor had crushed my esophagus and caused tons of damage. He flipped my stomach and reconnected what was left of my esophagus to it. I remained in the hospital for six days and left with a beautiful reminder that I am alive.

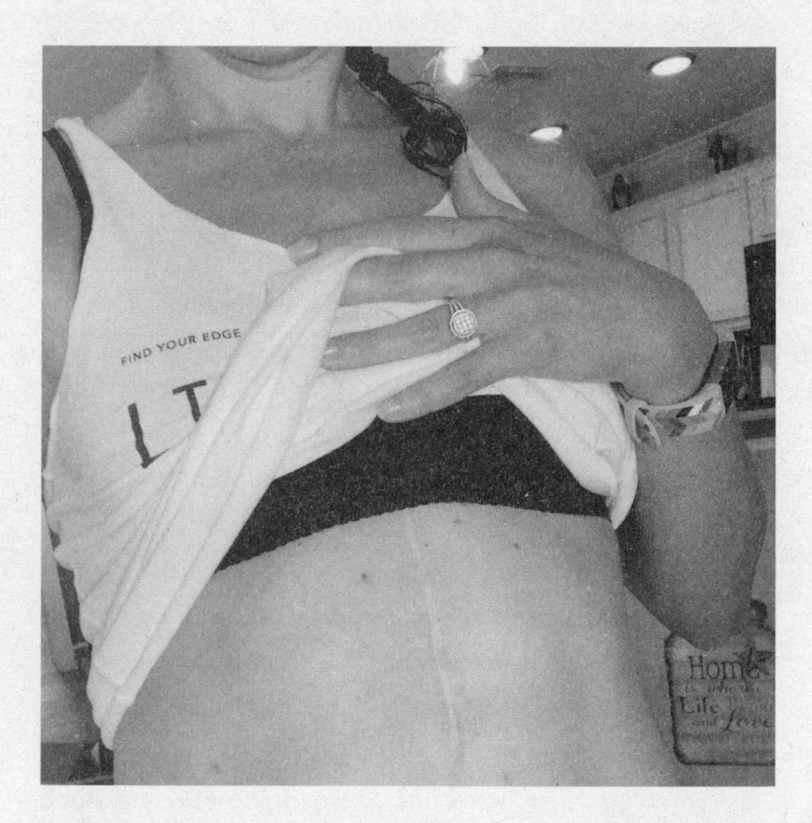

I had to have two more surgeries to correct complications, but I was one lucky son of a bitch.

My tumor had given me a massive gift. Colors were more vibrant, food tasted better, the freaking air smelled sweeter. I know that sounds like a bunch of bullshit, but this tumor gave me some perspective. It made me realize that control is an illusion, and yet I have the ability to choose and prioritize the parts and pieces of my life. I had my surgery in August of 2014, and on October 4, 2014, I made the first entry on my blog. I was no longer worried about what other people thought. I was no longer willing to sit on the sidelines of my life. I was going to do what I wanted to do. I was going to figure out what my purpose was. I knew I had married the right man. I was blessed with three amazing children. I needed to find myself again, and hold myself accountable to fulfilling my dreams and goals.

My tumor was a wake-up call. My tumor was a reminder that I am mortal. My tumor was a gift. I am truly #Blessed to have had this experience. My tumor made me realize that life is way too damn short to spend time with people I'd rather not. Life is way too short to try to please everyone. Life is way too short to give up dreams. We get one shot. My tumor made me realize that I had things to do. I have spent the past six years doing things I never thought possible. I managed to find myself. It has become my mission to talk about the realities of being a woman, wife, and mother. It is my mission to connect women, so that no one feels alone while in the trenches of parenting. It is my mission to make you laugh when you think you might cry. Don't get me wrong—crying can be nice too, but I much prefer laughing. We all need to laugh, because parenting is hard as fuck.

CHAPTER FOUR

Real Friends Are the Best Friends: Here's Why

In your 20s, the bar for friendship is low: you just want someone to hold your hair back when you've had too much tequila at a frat party. Once you have kids, you need something else: friends who will listen to your complaints about motherhood without judgment. What you absolutely don't need is a frenemy like Susan saying things like, "Looks like you forgot to put shoes on your son." Ya think so, Susan?! I can see he didn't put on his shoes and now we are walking into the grocery store, clearly defying the "No shirt, No shoes, No service" sign. This chapter will help you distinguish between real friends and the Susans of this world.

REAL FRIENDS CALL YOU ON YOUR BULLSHIT

When I was younger, I loved when my friends would compliment me. When I'd try on a piece of clothing that looked like crap and they'd tell me I looked great. When they'd take my side and tell me I was right, even when I wasn't. When they'd encourage me to do really stupid stuff that always ended in disaster. Now that I'm older, I see that those people weren't friends at all. Those people were buttholes. Because real friends tell you the truth. Real friends call you on your bullshit.

Real friends always . . .

1. Tell you when the pants you are wearing are way too tight and they show off every granny panty line in HD Real Time detail. You know, when your ass looks like a topographical map of the continental United States of America.

2. Scream "bullshit" when you are bold-faced lying. Not in front of the person you are going to lie to, but when the two of you are talking about it privately. A real friend will not call you out for a lie during said lie. She will wait and call your ass out in private.

3. Bring alcohol, chocolate, sweets, trash magazines, or a casserole when you are sick, had surgery, or had a really awful fight with your significant other. Nothing says "I love you, friend" like not having to make dinner, and who doesn't like a nice chicken and mushroom casserole? YUMMMMMMMMMM.

4. Tell you to just "stop" when you make a ridiculous excuse as to why you can't go somewhere or do something. They will force you to come out of your shell and experience new things.

5. Know when you are in an awful, nasty mood, and they won't make you go do something that you really, truly don't want to do. They might give you shit for it, but they will have your back.

6. Have your back. They will stand up for you when that nasty PTA Mom Susan talks smack about you at the '80s night mixer, and let her know that you are a force to be reckoned with.

7. Text you to check in and see how you are doing. They will then ask permission to call you, because they don't want to ambush you into a phone call like a monster.

8. Ignore your hellaciously loud screams over the phone when you are demanding that your children put on their shoes so you can go meet said friend for coffee.

9. Stay silent even when you are in the wrong when you are fighting with your spouse. When you are done ugly crying or yelling, they will help you see the other side of the story, so that you can find some perspective on the situation. Now, if your husband is truly being a butt munch, they will point that out and let you call him every name in the book.

10. Show up, each and every day. They are a piece of your soul.

REAL FRIENDS TEXT

Before I had kids, I remember talking on the phone to anyone and everyone. When my husband and I were dating, we would sit talking on the phone, watching television together. Yes, you read that right. We would sit on the phone and watch late-night TV together while saying, "You hang up—no, you hang up." If I were on the phone with him today and he said, "You hang up," it would take less than .000001 of a second for the call to be over.

You see, talking on the phone is cringe-worthy after having kids. It's like a weird mix of verbal diarrhea, shouting at kids to take their fingers out of their butts, and saying things like, "I forgot to get toilet paper again, DAMN IT!" Unless it is an emergency, phone calls don't happen anymore. The genius of texting is that you can answer a question without ever saying a word, which is great because the second you get on the phone, your kids can sense it and they begin to act like feral cats who just ingested a large quantity of crack cocaine.

If you are a phone call person, please know that people like me aren't trying to avoid talking to you. It's just that talking on the phone is impractical and creates more chaos in my world. Please don't get upset if you figure out that I have rejected your phone call. It most likely has nothing to do with you and everything to do with whether or not I am currently cleaning up poop, picking up Legos, or sweeping up glitter from an unauthorized craft project that my daughter secretly launched in her room unbeknownst to me. Also, can we all agree that glitter is the herpes of the arts-and-craft world? Texting gives me the opportunity to answer you—at my earliest convenience, mind you—and continue to shout at my children to "BRUSH YOUR TEETH" without your hearing me scream at them. It keeps the relationship more "breezy," if you will. No one, except my children, needs to hear that exceptionally shrill tone. Believe me, I am saving your hearing.

Don't get me wrong: I love to have conversations with my friends. I just prefer to do it in person, with a bottle of wine and no children. Texting is my daily lifeline in between girls' night out and bumping into each other at Target. Time with your friends is so necessary after having kids. It helps us remember who we were before having our delightful blessings. It might take 687 text messages to make plans to have a girls' night out, but it will totally be worth it. In the meantime, there's texting.

CAN WE GO BACK TO THE GOOD OL' DAYS WHEN WE COULD LIE TO OUR FRIENDS WITHOUT THEM FINDING OUT?

I am not the best of friends. I don't mean to be such an asshole, but it seems that I have a hard time with interpreting people's feelings and understanding the appropriate response. I truly have every intention of being there for my friends to the best of my abilities. However, I sometimes miss the friendship mark. I never do this out of malice; I am just a very forgetful person who is also exceptionally unorganized. You have to think of me as the Winn-Dixie of people—I'm getting better all the time, but clearly I am not there yet. For those of you who don't know what Winn-Dixie is, it is a grocery store, and yes, "Getting better all the time" is their brand tagline. Seriously, what the fuck? Just *be* better. However, I am a prime example that it clearly is easier said than done.

Back to what I was saying. My best friends went out of town for an overnight trip. I was supposed to feed and let their dog out while they were gone. It was 11 P.M. on the night I was supposed to let the dog out. Here is the text message conversation with my friend.

Trey: Hey. How are you?

Meredith: I'm good. What's up?

Trey: How was Paisley when you let her out? Was she good for you?

(At this point, I was realizing I had forgotten to let the dog out. An audible FUCK slipped out of my mouth. I paused Naked and Afraid *on my TV and began to think about my next move very carefully. Clearly, I decided to lie.)*

Meredith: She was great.

(I waited and watched the three blue dots indicating that Trey was texting me back.)

Trey: . . .

(This went on for a few minutes until finally his reply flashed on my phone screen.)

Trey: LIAR!!!! I didn't get a notification from my RING doorbell and there was no email from my security alarm system letting me know someone entered the house. You forgot to walk the dog. You promised you would walk her!

Meredith: I'm on my way now. This is really your fault. You didn't remind me to walk her.

Trey: Are you really blaming me for not reminding you to do the favor you promised to do?

Meredith: *Random emojis and GIF of a dancing dog*

We can no longer lie to our friends, our loved ones, or anyone, for that matter. We live in a time where technology is the biggest narc on the planet.

Thanks to text alerts, email notifications, and the green light that notifies all of your Facebook Friends that you are currently active and online, everyone knows what you are doing, where you are going, and how much you are spending on Oreos, Preparation H wipes, and wine. We can't lie about anything. I'm not saying I actively want to lie, but I'd like to have the option. Things were more innocent when we could lie about how much money we spent, or if we actually completed a favor a friend asked of us. Just sayin'.

I LOVE TEXTING, BUT I'M AN AWFUL TEXTER

I love texting. It is so wonderful to talk to people without actually talking to them. You can make plans (Who am I kidding? You make pretend plans that you are going to cancel because something will inevitably come up), get updates on gossip, and talk about the new digital series you are currently addicted to

(*Schitt's Creek*! People, it is the BEST!). Texting puts you in control. You can enter and exit the conversation at your leisure. You are the boss.

It has recently been brought to my attention that I am a terrible texter. I was unaware that there are rules to texting. A friend of mine sent me an article from *Entrepreneur* magazine as a joke, which claimed, "Although fast and convenient, texting brings about its own set of challenges. Words can be misinterpreted, messages can be incomplete and etiquette boundaries can be violated without your knowledge." The article outlined seven etiquette text rules that all texters should follow for successful communication.

The first rule was to consider your audience. Know the person you are engaging with. Apparently, I am too blunt when I text. Well, if I am texting with people, I know them. That means they know me. That means they know that I don't have time to bullshit. They should know that's the type of person I am and love me for me. If they don't, well, that's clearly on them.

The second rule was to communicate clearly. I stand firm in the fact that I communicate clearly. If someone texts me, "Dinner will be at 6:30. We are meeting at the restaurant," I will respond with "OK." I am not sure why it is necessary to elaborate on the fact that I understand that we are to meet at the restaurant at six thirty. A one-word response is all that is needed. I have been told that this response is off-putting and insinuates that I am angry. It really only implies that I understand dinner is at six thirty.

The third rule was to respond promptly. Well, I work all the time. I have three kids. I, despite what some of my family members think, do in fact have a full-time career even though that career is based in social media. I know I'm on Facebook a lot, but that is really my job. I spend my days cleaning, doing laundry, writing books, making and editing videos, picking up the kids from school, and being a badass motherfucker all at the same time. If I miss responding to your text message in a timely fashion, it really isn't personal. I probably saw the message pop up while I was replying to an email and then forgot to go back and reply to it. You will most likely only get an instant reply if I am actively on the toilet. It is pretty much the only time I am sitting still for more than 15 seconds. Yes, I do have my phone in my hands while I'm on the toilet. I don't care if you think that's gross.

The fourth piece of etiquette advice is to use symbols and emojis only when necessary. Well, that is ridiculous. I love emojis. I might be a super short, blunt texter, but watch out . . . I love to throw GIFs and emojis all over the place. It's your birthday, SWEET! I'm gonna send you a GIF of a chubby kid eating cake and dancing like nobody's watching. I'm sure that was offensive to some of you, but let's be honest, we all send that GIF, we just don't admit to it in a published book.

The fifth rule states that you shouldn't be long-winded. Well, that is super easy for me. I like to respond with one-word answers. However, I have an issue where I send my text messages one sentence at a time. It looks something like this.

Janet: BBQ is at 5PM on Sunday. See you there. I can't wait for the kids to swim! Have a great week.

Meredith: Sweet.

What should we bring?

Alcohol?

Fruit?

Chronic?

Just kidding about the weed.

Series of random emojis

BTW I can't swim but I'm pretty sure my kids can.

OK, sorry I made this awkward.

The sixth rule is to be patient. We need to be sensitive of others' time in waiting for a response. Well, that is just horse shit. I can take several days to reply to someone, but they'd better not pull that shit with me. If I text you, you'd better respond to me in a timely fashion. I have shit to do and if I asked you a question, I expect a response. I totally understand that this is a complete contradiction to my stance on rule three, but what can I say???

The final rule is to know when to end the conversation. Clearly, I have an issue with this one. I made things super awkward in the text exchange in rule number five. My text conversations usually end with me sending an inappropriate GIF or emoji, or a one-word response that leaves the recipient feeling emotionally scarred. Is all of this my fault? Probably. Am I willing to fix this? No. I want to want to be a better texter, but I don't foresee any actual changes being made. So, if you texted me and the conversation leaves you feeling unsatisfied, you are in good company. Just know that my heart was most likely in the right place. Winky face. Smiley face. Heart. Champagne bottle. GIF of a dog smiling.

EXPECTATION VERSUS REALITY FOR MAKING SIMPLE PLANS

When you have kids, making plans can go sideways really quickly. We all want to believe that when we have kids we won't allow our lives to drastically change. We will still make time for our friends. For our hobbies. For our spouses. For our careers. We are basically just ignorant and for the most part it isn't our fault. Before having kids, we were in charge of our lives. We decided where we went, when we went there, and what we were going to do when we got there. How on earth were we supposed to know that our entire lives were going to be uprooted and even the simplest event or task was going to require months of preplanning and strategic organization that could rival a covert military operation?

It is impossible to know what it is like to have kids prior to having kids. On top of that, even when you tell people what it is really like to have kids, they assume that won't happen to them. Why? We lie to ourselves because we always think we are going to be the exception, not the rule. Well, welcome to parenthood, where it takes months to plan a lunch date with a friend, because kids. It probably looks something like this:

You are in Target, standing in the under-five-dollar section at the front of the store. You have one kid in the cart. One kid is picking through the Paw Patrol sock bin, and the other kid is getting ready to put a bouncy ball in his mouth. Up walks a friend you haven't seen in months.

KAREN: Hey, girl! I haven't seen you in forever. How are things?

YOU: OH my gosh! Hey! I know. We are good. Busy, but good. How about you?

KAREN: Same! I needed toilet paper, but as you can clearly see, I picked up a few other things that weren't on my list. Damn that Joanna Gaines. Am I right?!?!?

YOU: I know. I know. I always say we only need three things and then we get in here and who can say no to the clearance rack?

KAREN: The kids look good. We should totally have a barbecue.

YOU: (*Becoming increasingly distracted as one of your kids is holding on to your leg and pulling down your yoga pants. Another kid is hitting the shopping cart into your heel, while the child in the cart is asking for an ICEE and a popcorn that you PROMISED ten minutes ago, and now you are the absolute worst mom ever.*) Yes! We totally need to do that. Text me this week and we will set it up!

KAREN: Sounds great! Talk soon!

You will most likely leave Target with every intention of making plans with Karen. You like Karen. You like barbecued ribs. It's a match made in heaven. A few days later, Karen texts you.

Karen: Hey! Will July 15 work for a BBQ?

You: (*You take a peek at your calendar.*) Oh no! That is no good for us. We have a dance recital that day. Will July 22 work for you guys?

Karen: Oh crap! We have a soccer tournament that weekend. How about August 10?

You: That is no good for us. We have a family gathering. How about August 15?

Karen: NOPE! *Mad emoji face* We have a baseball tournament. How about September 2?

You: UGH! We are out of town for Labor Day.

You will do this for about five more minutes until you realize that you can potentially meet up for a barbecue in the year 2027. Odds are you have a better chance at meeting up randomly at Target long before you will actually make plans together. I know we need to make time for our friends and have a social life. Friends really and truly are important, but with a bunch of kids, work, life, and everything else, it can be a huge pain in the ass to actually make concrete plans.

A few years ago, I decided to take a different approach to making plans with friends. I now let friends know what our plans are in case they can also make it there as well. I would shoot a text and say, "Hey! We are going to the movies Saturday at 11AM. If you can make it, great. If not, we totally get it." I have found that being very open-ended can be the best way to make plans when everyone is so busy. No one is upset if it doesn't work out, and when it does work out, everyone is happy to see each other. Friendship looks different during parenthood, and that is all good.

PLEASE TELL ME WHEN MY KID IS ACTING LIKE A DICKHEAD. PARENTING IS HARD AND I NEED HELP.

I know, as parents, we want to believe that our children are always making good choices. We try to model good behavior, but at times we fail. We work hard to make sure they feel loved and yet sometimes we fail. We try to let them know that they mean the world to us without turning them into entitled tiny assholes. It is a really, really tough job, and we need our friends to help us out and call our kids on their sketchy behavior.

As a former teacher, I have had way too many parent–teacher conferences where I called in a parent to explain a situation with a child and the parent's response was, "Not my baby. My child wouldn't do that." What I wanted to say to that response was this: "Well, your child did do it and she was acting like a dickhead. She made a poor choice and it happens, but we need to correct it. She needs to know what is acceptable behavior, and it is your job and my job to help this child find the proper path. Why on earth would I lie about this? It's not like I make extra money holding parent–teacher conferences with parents who think I am lying about the stupid shit their kids do." Now, as a result of wanting to keep my job, I never said this in a parent–teacher conference. I am no longer a teacher, so yeah, I just said that.

Please do not think that your child can do no wrong. All kids make mistakes. All kids slip up. They are humans after all. I taught thousands of kids over the 13 years I spent in the public school system. They were all special, but they were by no means all saints. Fun fact: it was really hard to pick names for my children, because every time my husband or I would pick a name, we would each say, "No, we can't name him that. I had a kid who was a real ass with that name. What else you got?" So in the end, be a friend. Call out my kids when they are being a dickhead and I will do you the same favor. As a former teacher, I find it pretty easy to talk directly to kids about their behavior. I am sure if you don't have a ton of experience with other people's kids, that might be a bit alarming to you. If so, talk directly to your friend. Tell her what you are seeing and remind her that you are filling her in out of love. It will make a difference in the long run.

We were traveling as a family to my niece's Sweet Sixteen birthday party last year, when something really cool happened. We had to fly out of Miami to the Caribbean island of St. Croix. We all boarded the plane, and our seats were separated from our kids'. My husband thought he booked our three kids in the seats behind us, but they were about four or five rows back. I was a complete nervous wreck about this. We sat down and my husband went back and got the kids situated in their seats. He made sure they all had headphones and then, I'm sure, attempted to instill the fear of God in them with a well-meaning message of "I swear to God, if I have to come back here, I will lose my shit." I am not 100 percent certain that he said this, but I know him well enough to know that was probably what went down.

About 20 minutes into the flight, I looked back and they were all quiet. Thirty minutes later, still quiet. At one point I saw my daughter go to the bathroom, then my son. About 15 minutes before we landed, I got up to go to the bathroom. There were two flight attendants sitting in their jump seats and one of them said, "Are those three kids in row 15 yours?" I took a deep breath while thinking to myself, "For. The. Love. What did they do?" Which is usually my reaction anytime someone asks me if "those kids" are my kids. She continued, saying, "I just need to tell you that your kids are the sweetest kids I have ever encountered. I have been a flight attendant for 15 years and they are just wonderful. Fantastic manners! Just great kids!" I felt a wave of relief rush over me. I was proud and excited. It was so wonderful to be told that those children who scream like they are being attacked by hyenas when asked to pick up their toys can be delightful while in public.

It is easy to forget how great our kids are when we tend to see them at their worst, day in and day out. We see the tantrums. We see the refusals to get dressed for school. We see the food they spit out when we slave over a hot stove for 30 minutes. We see the worst because they love us, trust us, and we are their safe place. We work really hard to instill good manners, good morals, and good behavior. Times like that flight prove my lessons weren't lost on deaf ears.

Conversely, if my kids are acting like dickheads, I also want to know about it. My children are not angels, and if you are a teacher or administrator at my child's school, a friend of mine, a Target employee, a coach, or a member of my church, please, for the love of all things holy, tell me that my kid is acting out. Don't sugarcoat it. Don't lie. Don't look the other way. It is my job to make sure that my children are held accountable and I need lots of help with that. I need the people in my life to help me out, because raising children to become good human beings is a really fucking hard task.

AN ODE TO THE MOM IN MY KID'S CLASS WHO BRINGS IN SNACKS SO I CAN BRING IN THE NAPKINS

I have never been the class mom. I am rarely on time to school events. I often forget about them until the night before. I don't bake. I can't craft. I usually opt out of the school fund-raiser if at all possible. I'm like a fish out of water when it comes to PTA meetings and school functions. I was so uncomfortable at my kids' school play a few years back that I considered getting up and walking out. I hate interpretive dance, and there was a scene in the play where this kid was turning into a butterfly, and I was ready to lose my shit. As a logical adult, I knew I couldn't get up and leave, but every fiber of my being wanted to run for the hills.

Back to my point. I am no June Cleaver. Clearly. However, I want to thank all of the PTA and crafty moms (the moms who truly love to create these magical items for their children's classes, and aren't the judgy Susans of the world who just want to stick it to us) out there who sign up to bring the baked goods and make the papier-mâché dragons for the school play. You make it possible for me to sign up for the napkins and feel like I am making somewhat of a contribution, no matter how small. We need you! Our kids need you! You are amazing and I truly want to say thank you!

When I was in the trenches of parenting, when my kids were much younger, I used to resent these moms. I would snicker as I saw them bring in the homemade cupcakes. I would doubt myself and worry I wasn't a good enough mom. I would play that awful comparison game. The game you never, ever win. I would sign up for napkins, but bring in those napkins with a hot, fresh side of spite. I was dropping off my kids at day care one morning when a mom came in with the Halloween cupcakes for the class. I opened the door for her and immediately felt shame as I held my pack of napkins. She smiled at me and I said, "Nice cupcakes." She smiled back and said that she had been up all night because she burned one batch and dropped another on the floor. She wanted to surprise her daughter with these cupcakes, but they had almost broken her spirit. I was shocked. She wasn't making the cupcakes to stick it to me. She was simply being the best mom that she could be.

I realize now that I was wrong to judge the moms who nailed it with their classroom volunteer hours and perfectly crafted nutritious and allergy-friendly treats. You gave me the opportunity to be the mom who I am. I am Napkin Mom and I am really proud of that. I know it might seem like a small part to play, but it is the part that I am best suited for. Also, kids spill a ton of shit and we need lots of napkins to clean up their messes. We are all good at something, but if you've seen me bake, clearly, I'm not good at everything. No one is. So why as moms do we assume we will be good at all of the parts of motherhood? Because we play the comparison game until we want to run away or hit Susan's car with a bat. Luckily, I learned that being Napkin Mom is perfect for me. So, thank you to every mom who does what she is good at so Napkin Moms have a seat at the table.

CHAPTER FIVE

My Husband's Love Language Is Sex (and Other Things I've Learned in 17 Years of Marriage)

According to Gary Chapman's *The 5 Love Languages*, my love language is "acts of service," like when I cook a meal for my husband or remember to iron his favorite shirt for a date night. It's my way to show him how much I love him. My husband's love language, on the other hand, is "physical touch." This means having sex or holding hands. My husband does not want to hold my hand unless that is followed by having sex. He has also never given me a back rub that ended as a back rub. Back rubs always end as front rubs and then sex. So, let's talk about sex, shall we?

CAN I SCHEDULE SOME SEX, PLEASE?

I always laugh when my husband tries to compare our sex life now to back before we had kids. If you ask me, that is kind of like comparing apples to a car. You thought I was going to say "oranges," but an orange and an apple are still fruits and probably have way too many commonalities. Let's take a look at sex before kids and sex after kids.

Sex Before Kids: Privacy

You can do it anywhere and at any time in your home. You are literally the only people who live there. You can do it on the kitchen table if you want, but make sure to properly sanitize prior to serving food or entertaining guests. You have the ability to be spontaneous. You have the ability to leave the door open. You have the ability to scream and moan, and just be in the moment without the fear of being walked in on by someone who just wet the bed.

Sex After Kids: Privacy

You are never alone. Someone is always trying to get into your room or into your bed. It can be difficult to snag some "sexy time" with a bed-wetting toddler in between you and your husband. There is no such thing as privacy any longer.

Sex Before Kids: Energy

You had so much energy and free time. Before having kids, you had time to be bored. Let that marinate for a hot second. You used to be bored. Bahahahahahahahahahahahahaha. You also used to think you were busy. You had increased energy because you actually got to sleep at night without interruptions. With more energy, the thought of touching your husband's penis is more of a pleasure than a chore. It is amazing what happens if you have eight hours of sleep.

Being spontaneous is simple when you don't have kids. You aren't bound to other people's schedules, so you don't have to plan your sex life.

Sex After Kids: Energy

The level of exhaustion you feel after having children is unimaginable. You have never felt so tired in your entire life. You used to think you were tired, but then you had kids. You were so dumb before.

Sex Before Kids: Touching

Before having kids, you had so much time on your hands, meaning, your hands were free to do things like touch your husband's penis. You would spend time thinking about sex. Talking with your friends about the sex. Imagining how amazing the sex would be. You were also more bendy and flexible. You were excited to be touched. You wanted to be touched. It was a pleasurable experience that most often ended with your "O" face and not your "OH MY GOD, A KID JUST WALKED IN" face.

Sex After Kids: Touching

You have been touched all day long. Literally someone has been hanging on you, your breasts, your hair, your leg, your back ALL. DAY. LONG. When your husband comes home to greet you with a "stiff" surprise, it is really hard to want to be touched.

Sex Before Kids: The Vagina

It was tight. It was impressive. It was in peak condition. It was red-carpet ready. I can go on and on. The pre-baby vagina is something to be cherished.

Sex After Kids: The Vagina

Once you have a vaginal delivery, there is absolutely no going back. It will never look the same; at least mine doesn't. My poor vagina was torn, ripped, and basically dragged behind a truck for miles down an unpaved country road. Let's take a moment of silence for all the broken vaginas out in the world. Your pre-baby vagina was like a pretty sports car. It was shiny and new. Your post-baby vagina is more of a reliable minivan. Don't worry—the minivan can have lots of fun, I promise.

As your kids get older and you are less like a zombie, your sex life will improve. Plus, as you get older, you will know what you like and don't like. Be vocal and tell your partner what you need in the bedroom. Make your sexy time count. If you want him to pull your hair, just ask. My husband stopped me one morning and said, "I need a quickie. I had a sex dream about you and we gotta do it. Meet you in the bathroom in two minutes." He was very specific with what he needed. Women, we CAN and SHOULD be as crystal clear as our partners. It will definitely lead to more smiles.

I WOULD BE THE INITIAL SUSPECT IN MY SPOUSE'S MISSING PERSON CASE, AND HERE'S WHY

My husband is a wonderful man. He is also a slob. I love him each and every day, but there are plenty of times when I do not like him. Before you think I am an awful person, I guarantee you there are plenty of days when he does not like me either. Marriages sometimes involve mutual disdain, and that is okay. It truly is. It is not easy to live with another person and share all of your things. I mean, consider all the things you actually share with your spouse:

1. **The Marriage Bed:** The place where you lay your head down and close your eyes is shared with another person. The place where you are the most vulnerable. I mean, he could roll over at any given moment and try to smother you. More likely, he will roll over and attempt to deliver a package that you have received before on many, many occasions.

2. **The Bathroom:** The place where you poop is also the place where your spouse poops. Poop is awful. It smells terrible, and if your husband is like my husband, he likes to poop naked. It is a legit thing that people do. I have no idea why, but someone somewhere started this movement, and each day there are new members in the naked pooper society. Walking in and seeing my naked husband taking a crap is never a mood enhancer. Maybe it's just me.

3. The Bathroom Sink: This is its own separate item on the list because the bathroom counter and sink are serious. My husband is a very messy counter partner. He is always leaving his used Q-tips on the counter and beard trimmings in the bathroom sink, along with massive globs of toothpaste. I personally think that leaving disgusting shaving trimmings in the bathroom sink should be an arrestable offense.

4. Hairbrush: I have found beard hair in my hairbrush, because I apparently have to share my hairbrush with my bald husband. Yes, my husband is bald, but he does have a glorious beard, which he brushes with my hairbrush. I just love when I find his beard hairs in my hair later on in the day.

5. The Driveway: This might sound funny to you, but, like our bed, our driveway has his and hers sides. I like to park on the left-hand side of the driveway. It is my side. I claimed it and it should be respected. My husband knows I prefer the left side, yet I will come home to find him on my side of the driveway. Why? Seriously, why would anyone do that? When you claim a side, your partner should respect that. If this sounds petty to you, please know that I don't care. It is a thing and it irks me.

6. Treats: When I go to the grocery store, I will sometimes buy myself a treat. I will place said treat in the fridge only to later discover that the treat was eaten by my husband. I sometimes consider labeling my food like people in office buildings.

7. **Love:** We share so much mind-numbing, gag-inducing love for each other that it is nauseating. Wait, that is probably just Susan's marriage. Most marriages will and should include love, but they will also include arguments, periods of silence, periods of resentment, periods of joy and laughter, and periods of relationship repair. I can tell you that during our 17-year marriage, we have had massive arguments and moments where I was so worried that I would lose him that I could feel my heart break inside of my chest.

Marriage is all about sharing and most of the time that is great, but we are all humans and it can be taxing. So don't let the internet or relatives in your life get you down on your marriage. Marriage is tough, and it rarely looks like a wedding magazine cover photo. If you want a true snapshot of love in a marriage, picture this: My husband really knew I loved him when I had to "glove up" and give him an anal suppository after his appendectomy. Now, that is love. Not the type of unforgettable moment I was hoping for, but still, love.

MOVIE SHOWER SEX IS STUPID

I don't get to watch a ton of television, but when I do, I really love it. It is my favorite way to zone out and not think about anything. I love making my mind go blank and watching my favorite actors and actresses act out a story for my entertainment. There's a certain kind of sex scene, though, that always makes me laugh. I'm talking, of course, about shower sex. Truth: NO ONE HAS SHOWER SEX LIKE THAT!!!!

Think about it. Seriously, think back to every shower sex scene you have seen on TV and in the movies. Have you ever had epic shower sex like they do in the movies? If so, I want you to call me immediately—I need every detail. If not, continue reading why I think it is totally bullshit and causes people to have warped expectations about sex.

In the movies, the shower is big enough for both people to adequately fit and it's so clean it shines bright like Rihanna's diamond. There is one shampoo bottle, one conditioner bottle, and one massage oil bottle. All expensive organic brands with pretty pink and teal labels. The shower probably has a bench seat so that lovers can recline in some tantric sex position while the massaging showerhead blasts them with pulsing water vibrations. The kind of water vibrations that can keep you in the mood all night long. Sometimes the extremely thin, attractive, athletic-looking couple is so hot to trot for each other, they get into the shower with their clothes on. Yes, that's right. They jump into the shower with their jeans on and somehow, only explained by their beliefs in black magic, they are able to sexily pull the jeans off each other in one fell swoop. The showerhead seems to spray them evenly, water flowing over them in just the right places so as to not hinder their epic make-out session, which obviously includes French kissing (that means tongue kissing). You will see steamy hand and ass prints sliding down the door in slow motion. The steam continues to billow out the top of the shower like a forest fire. Eventually two simultaneous erotic scream-moans are heard when the epic sex has commenced.

I have never had epic movie-scene shower sex, but I have most definitely had real married shower sex. It usually looks like this: "Hey, I haven't showered in a week and I have about seven minutes until I need to switch this load of laundry, and I have a new episode of *Grey's Anatomy* that I want to watch tonight, so if you want to do it, we need to do it now." My husband usually drops his pants immediately and pushes me into our milk-carton-sized shower, which is filled with toys, razors, children's bathing suits, beach floats, empty shampoo bottles, and a body loofa sponge that should never, ever be used again. It's basically now a science experiment. The showerhead sprays on my husband while I freeze. I am usually attempting to wash my hair and brush my teeth at the same time. I usually say, "Are you almost done?" about three times, while also saying, "Man, we are wasting a lot of water." I have a handicap bar in my shower that I usually hit my head on at least once during the magical lovemaking session. At this point one of our children usually enters and asks why both Mom and Dad are in the shower, to which I reply, "I'm conserving water—we gotta look out for Mother Earth." To which they reply, "Mom, I've never seen you recycle." "FOR THE LOVE OF ALL THINGS HOLY! GET OUT OF HERE SO I CAN FINISH YOUR FATHER AND WATCH MY TV SHOW TONIGHT IN PEACE AND QUIET!"

My point is very simple and clear. No one has a sex life like those we see in the movies, not even Susan and her husband. I am positive of that. So, if you are like me and you are using shower sex to gain an extra 15 minutes of sleep, please know you are not alone, it is normal, and your sex life is just fine. If Chris Pratt or Ryan Reynolds want to prove me wrong, they can call me. Both are on my laminated list.

REASONS I'VE USED TO GET OUT OF SEX

Picture it: It's a school night. You have on your Christmas jammies even though it's May. It's been a really long day. You went grocery shopping. You had to take the dog to the vet. You did 37 loads of laundry. You walk into your bedroom and get all snuggly under the covers. You turn on the television and put on the latest episode of *Grey's Anatomy*. Your hair is in a bun and you already have your retainer or mouth guard in. All of a sudden your husband crawls into bed and you find his hand inside your pants. What do you do?

Here are some of my favorite go-to responses when my husband is in the mood and I'm not feeling it.

1. I'm a bit gassy. I had tacos for lunch. (True story)

2. I have a headache. (I have three kids . . . I definitely had a headache.)

3. I have a bad case of swamp ass. (This is legitimately a thing. Swamp ass occurs in the southern parts of the United States as well as countries located in continents that have high humidity. Swamp ass is basically when you sweat nonstop and your crotch-er-ler region gets raw and rashy from being sweaty all day. It's the pits.)

4. We did it yesterday. ('Cuz we did. So stop it.)

5. I just washed the sheets. (Why is it wrong to want to sleep on clean sheets??? At least for one night.)

6. I dreamt you had an affair and I'm not over that yet. (That bitch Susan was trying to get my man again.)

7. I wore the kids like a coat today—can I have a pass, please? (No one wants to be touched all day long.)

8. I have cramps. (I had to stop using this one in November 2018, as I had a hysterectomy. Super sad about that.)

9. I'M SO TIRED. (Also a true story. I did like 18 loads of laundry, cleaned the house, had seven conference calls, took the kids to practice, and chased the dog down the street in the rain.)

10. How about a blow job instead? (This one always works, and subsequently gets me out of having sex. I'm not a complete bitch.)

I do not use excuses every time my husband initiates sex. I love having sex with my husband, but my husband wants to have sex all the time. He equates the act of sex as a way for us to connect and how he shows me that he loves me. I know he thinks his penis is a present, but I can think of a few other presents that I would love . . . perhaps some help with the laundry, dishes, or toilet cleaning. All of these things would most likely get him direct access to pound town.

MARRIAGE ISN'T EASY; STOP THINKING IT SHOULD BE

Marriage, much like parenting, is something you can't understand until you go through it. We all think we know what to expect, but I promise you truly don't. I married my husband when I was 23 and he was 24. I can tell you that today, as I'm 40 and he 41, we are not those people. We have been through a lot and have changed over the years. It is impossible not to change, and if we are being honest, we *should* change. Two of the big myths that we need to bust as a society are that marriage fixes problems and that if you are in love, it should be easy.

When you first get married, you think your spouse can

walk on water. You are so in love and you think the honeymoon will never end. It does end. It's supposed to end. It's a stage or phase of marriage, and you have to move past it. I think sometimes we fight to reinvent the honeymoon phase, and we end up setting unrealistic expectations for ourselves and our spouse.

My husband and I were in a bit of a funk last year. The stress of everyday life was wearing on both of us. We hadn't really been connecting.

I wanted to make sure he knew how much I love him. I would make grand plans in my mind, like *after I pick the kids up from school I will stop at the store and get something special for dinner. I will prepare a beautiful, elegant, romantic meal. I will make sure the kids go to bed early and we can snuggle on the couch and gaze into each other's eyes, until we both fully realize how lucky we are to have each other. The night will end with amazing sex and a complete feeling of oneness.*

But reality would get in the way every time. I would pick up the kids from school and they would fight nonstop in the car. We would stop at the grocery store and I would have to whisper-scream at them to stop putting food into the cart. When we arrived home, the house would always be a disaster. Whenever I asked my husband to do the dishes before I left, SHOCKER, he didn't do them. I'd cook dinner, but there were always 1,000 things going on with the kids, and I would get distracted and burn the chicken or otherwise derail the entire meal. I'd usually scream for approximately 30 minutes for the kids to shower and get ready for bed. The bedtime routine would take about an hour, as every child would need something. By the time I could finally sit on the couch with my husband, the last thing I'd want to do is snuggle, let alone look into his eyes. The same eyes that refused to look at the dishes that needed to be done, which I ended up doing. He would then make an advance, and we would be interrupted by a dehydrated child who desperately needed a glass of water.

Does any of this sound familiar? I find that I do this to myself often when it comes to my marriage. I build it up in my mind and then I am crushed when reality hits. It is so easy to paint the picture that we want to materialize, but it is so hard to make that reality happen. I'm not saying that we have to lower our expectations, I'm simply saying we need to be honest about our expectations. I know how rough the day gets once I pick the kids up from school. It is a nonstop cycle of homework, practices, fighting, meals, showers, more fighting over what TV show they are going to watch, and the struggle that is bedtime.

I'm sure my husband has expectation-versus-reality moments with me as well. I am positive that my husband would love it if I would ask him to take me to Home Depot so we can work on some home renovation project together. He would be so fucking jazzed if I asked him to teach me how to hold a drill or use a wrench. However, the reality is clear: I have no desire to do these things. Like none. I hate home renovation projects. They actually make me anxious and angry.

Living with another person is hard. Living with children is hard. Our expectation is that because we are living with loved ones it is going to be easy and wonderful and like a scene from

The Sound of Music. In reality, our lives resemble more of a mix of *Games of Thrones* and *House of Cards*, with a side of *Shameless*.

The point is pretty simple. Marriage is tough. Raising kids is tough. When we stop to reflect on our lives we usually think, "Should life really be this much of a fucking circus?" Sometimes the simple answer is yes. As a wife, mother, business owner, and friend, I have to please a lot of people. I have to show up and be involved. I have to give even when I don't receive. It can be thankless at times and mind-numbing, but it's that way for the majority of people. With all that said, that doesn't mean we don't find joy each and every day. We find the happy. We do our best to remember that it's all worth it. Obtaining anything of value requires hard work and dedication. Staying married and raising kids are two of the most stressful things we can do in our lives. It takes daily effort and energy; it simply is not going to be easy. No relationship worth having is easy. I might want to run away once a week and hit my husband with a baseball bat on occasion, but I would put my life on the line for my family.

THINGS I LIE TO MY HUSBAND ABOUT

Before you get your panties in a bunch, let me explain a few things. I believe you need to be honest with your spouse. However, we all tell a few white lies here and there. I fully believe that some lies are not only acceptable but necessary to keep the peace in a marriage, while others are completely off limits, much like Mommy's secret stash of dark chocolate peanut butter cups.

I will touch the thermostat and then say I didn't touch it. He gets very cranky when I touch it, but sometimes it needs to be adjusted. I'm an adult, damn it. I lie because I don't want to talk about the freaking thermostat. I enjoy keeping the house at 74 degrees while wearing a sweater. What can I say, I am a bit of a contradiction.

Prior to 2018 when my husband started grocery shopping for the household, I used to lie about how much I spent at the grocery store. I had a hard time staying on the budget he set up, so I would pay for some of the bill with cash. Yup, I said it. Grocery shopping for a household of five isn't cheap, and we always disagreed on a "want" versus a "need." Ice cream, for example. I both "want" and "need" it. This got tricky with the invention of credit card alerts. I was standing at the cashier paying for the groceries when my husband called and asked me why I spent $275 at the grocery store. I told him I didn't and he said, "I just got a text alert with the total you spent." Well, SON OF A BITCH. I can't even lie about this anymore. The damn credit card companies rat my ass out before I even get home.

Anytime my husband asks if I read a bill or letter that came in the mail, I say yes, but we both know that was a bold-faced lie. I hate looking through the bills. The "important" pile of bills is a massive stack; it brings me crippling anxiety to even look at it. When I say I "looked" at the bills, it basically means I took the mail in from the mailbox and placed it in the stack of unopened angry red envelopes. Thankfully, we now have everything set up on auto pay. I continue to take the mail in from the mailbox and set it in a pile, and we both ignore the stack.

I lie when I tell my husband that I don't care where we go to dinner. I want to not care, but when he tells me where he wants to go, I obviously don't want to go there. So, much like every couple on the planet, we play this game until he is yelling and I am upset because he can't telepathically know where I want to go to dinner. In all honesty, I don't really know where I want to go to dinner, I just know where I *don't* want to go to dinner. Does that make sense?

Anytime my husband asks if I am listening to him, I say yes, but most likely I wasn't. My brain is a constant swirl of thoughts, and they are very, very loud. I have the attention span of a squirrel on crack cocaine, so it can be difficult for me to keep and hold conversations. I am pretty sure he is guilty of this same lie, because he never has any idea of what I was talking about either.

THINGS I WILL NEVER LIE TO MY HUSBAND ABOUT

Saying "I love you." Every single time I say those words, I mean it. My husband is a good man who has been super supportive of my dreams, both personally and professionally. He is my rock and I will always love him. If we are annoyed with each other, I will say, "I love you more." And he will say, "I know."

Saying "I'm sorry." I only apologize when I am actually sorry. If I'm not sorry, I will not say it. I don't want him to give me a fake apology, so I will not give him one. I used to say sorry to avoid or end an argument. I don't do that any longer. I found that when I apologized when I didn't mean it, I would carry resentment, and we would fight about the same things over and over again.

Saying "I was wrong." For the first 14 years of our marriage, I was really bad at this. As a very competitive person, I felt like the first ten years of our marriage were spent keeping score. I didn't want to admit being wrong because that meant I was losing. I still struggle at times. I don't like being wrong. We have grown a lot since I got sick in 2014. We have learned to become teammates instead of competitors. I have learned that when I am wrong, I need to admit it and move on. However, if I don't believe I am in the wrong, I try to talk it out with my husband, to figure out his feelings about the situation and see his point of view.

My feelings. When I am upset, I tell him. I do my best to be super specific, as my husband has a hard time with feelings. When my husband pisses me off, I tell him at that exact moment. I don't want to collect resentments and pull them up at a later date to fight about.

Needing help. I used to make my list and pretend that I could do it all—the house, the kids, work, life. I needed to be everyone's everything, at all times. Not only is that impossible, but it quickly builds resentment and causes people to keep score in their relationships. I pretended to not need any help for the first 12 years of our marriage. It caused me to be bitter and resentful, and in turn, soured our marriage. Once I opened up about how overwhelmed I was, it was like a light switch went off in my husband's head. He was finally able to see what I needed, because I was finally able to tell him. He is not a mind reader and neither am I. We need to help each other in order to have stability in our relationship and family.

Marriage is tricky, but if you put your best foot forward, you can navigate the bumpy waters. There are days I look at my husband and think, "I need you to go away for a few hours . . . maybe days." There are times when I think, "I am the luckiest woman on the planet. I don't deserve him." Finding the middle ground keeps us going. I know I sometimes drive him nuts, but my true intention is to always love him, stand by him, and take care of him. I know he loves me too, so we work each day to stay afloat. It's not sexy. It's not the stuff they make movies about, but it's reality. And the last time I checked, we aren't in a Tom Hanks and Meg Ryan rom-com; marriage is more like a battle scene out of *Gladiator*.

ROMANCE ISN'T ALWAYS ROSES. CLEANING A TOILET WILL MAKE MY PANTIES DROP.

I am the least sentimental female on the planet. We recently did a 23 and Me genetic test and I have almost 100 more Neanderthal markers than my husband. Apparently, my lack of sentimentalism is straight-up genetic. I almost feel vindicated.

I am not a fan of Valentine's Day either. I personally think that Valentine's Day was created by the greeting card companies in order to boost the GDP. It then became a massive holiday where you have to prove your undying love for your special person on February 14 so that person knows you are committed. If you ask me, it is simply ridiculous. Now, I know some of you are going to say that you love Valentine's Day and I need to shut the fuck up, and I hear you. If you love Valentine's Day, I think you should celebrate it and enjoy every second of it. I simply refuse to participate.

My husband has always been the better gift giver over the years. We don't exchange gifts often, but when we do, he out-gifts me. He has always been more sentimental. He is a loving husband. However, I lack the romance-and-lace genetic marker, and his gestures tend to be lost on me. I am the first one to admit that I am emotionally stunted, so when I receive a very emotionally charged gift, I become uncomfortable. The time my husband framed a magazine that I was on the cover of, I made a face that resembles Chandler's photo face from *Friends*. You know the face. You are trying to smile but you smile too big and all of your teeth are showing. You start to look like some kind of startled animal that is at the beginning of a panic attack. Your eyes are big and the proper words escape you. Anyway, the point is, romance and sentiment escape me.

One time I bought lingerie to say "I'm sorry" to my husband. I assumed this was a traditional and sentimental way to show him that I was sorry and I do in fact love him. I put it on and walked into the bedroom. My husband was lying in bed. I walked over and locked the bedroom door. I began to strut over to the bed. In my head, my strut was sexy. Something you would see on the Victoria's Secret runway. However, my strut resembled something more along the lines of a male gorilla approaching a bunch of bananas across the jungle in the Congo. I jumped onto the bed like a feline on crack cocaine and pushed him down, while trying to move my head from side to side, making confused moaning sounds. Mind you, in my head I was the sexiest person on the planet in that moment. My husband was a good sport and after we did the deed, he told me how awkward I'd looked. We laughed about it, because honestly, being sexy is not my thing. I'm comfortable in my skin; however, my skin is more of a sweatpants and "you want a blow job?" kind of sexy.

I might not understand or be comfortable with traditional romance, but I do know what makes my panties drop. I love when my husband helps around the house without being asked. Yup, that's what turns on my engine. If I see my husband wash a dish without being prompted. If he buys me edible cookie dough at the grocery store. If he spends the evening playing outside with the kids so I can work on video editing or writing a book. When he is attentive to what I need, I want to jump on him like a Ugandan gorilla and go primitive ape on his ass. I am less about flash and more about "Hot damn, you took out the trash!" I have hit a point in my life where things are simply things. His acts of understanding are what make me hot and bothered. Him knowing I am out of coffee filters and bringing home a Coke because I had a stressful day are what make me feel loved and supported.

For me, my husband pitching in is catnip. I am high-strung and high anxiety. I am a list maker, and when he checks something off my list, I want to touch his penis more. My point, which seems to have gone rather sideways, is that sexy comes in all packages. It's not always roses; it could very well be cleaning a toilet. Romance changes over the years of marriage and in this season of our wedded bliss, I drop my drawers for thoughtful chores. What can I say, I am a classy lady.

CHAPTER SIX

Anxiety and Motherhood Go Hand in Hand: Enjoy!

I remember the first time I held my firstborn son in my arms. It was the most amazing and horrifying moment of my life. I was now responsible for another living, breathing, crying human being. It was at that precise moment that my "momxiety" kicked in. "Momxiety" is a constant feeling of forgetting something while simultaneously completing a task, while also worrying that you are also going to ruin everyone's life for all eternity. "Momxiety" is exacerbated by the demands of life, family, people in general, and all of the crap that we are expected to do each and every day of our lives.

SHHH . . . CAN YOU HEAR THAT?

Before having kids, I had no idea how beautiful and awesome a relatively "quiet" mind was. Once you become a mom, there is no quiet to be found. Your house is noisy, your thoughts are noisy, even the delightful sound of birds chirping is now like a jackhammer to the temple. I haven't had a "quiet" mind in a while, but I dream about it. At least I try to dream about it, but most of my dreams are filled with anxiety-riddled lists of things I didn't get done during the day. Even in my sleep I swear I can hear my kids asking for a snack, asking where their shoes are, asking for me to change the channel. Sometimes I wonder how long the "quiet" will evade me. I mourn the quiet. I try to think back to the last time I enjoyed the quiet, but I can't remember.

It never fails that when I talk about this, someone always comments that I will miss the chaos someday soon. I am positive that they are correct that I will miss this when my children are grown and have flown the coop, but right now my mind is a very noisy place. It is filled with doctors' appointments, birthday party invites, PTA fund-raiser requests, work emails, and trying to remember the last time I mopped; the anxiety builds like millions of Lego bricks being stacked, one on top of another, teetering on the brink of collapse.

My anxiety was like a bonus gift when I started having children. It was like, "Congratulations on having a baby! Now you get to worry about everything and anything for the rest of your life!" I try my hardest to keep the evil anxiety demons at bay, but at 3 A.M. they sneak back in and make themselves at home.

Seriously, I had no idea how noisy a mind could be. I think about conversations I had 20 years ago, bruised relationships, my daughter's last gymnastics competition, if my youngest son will ever find someone to marry, when my dog will die, if my husband loves me like he used to, what we should have for dinner. It can be crippling at times.

Even if I steal ten minutes of quiet, my mind destroys that. Sometimes my mind drifts to Susan. I lie there quietly thinking about the comment she posted on the Facebook post where I talked about how I yelled at my kids today:

> You are a mom . . . learn to communicate . . . or don't have kids . . . Constantly yelling or using that as "How I communicate" is a cop-out. Glad you get to blow off steam screaming . . . but it doesn't help the kid or situation. You have failed as a parent. Hope you're happy.

I lie there and think about how I want to reply to Susan. I type the message in my head and it goes like this:

> Susan, thank you so much for your comment. I really appreciate that you pointed out I am failing my children and that I shouldn't have had kids. You are just such a delight and a light of hope in this universe. I wish I could be more like you, but I hate you, so I am going to pass. Best wishes on figuring out how to be less of a douche-canoe.

Sadly, I never type things. So, I continue to battle my anxiety and resting bitch face each and every day. I wake tired from the middle-of-the-night struggles, get the kids ready for school, become a referee as my kids get into the minivan, threaten to turn around 15 times on the way to the drop-off lane, watch the other moms who had enough dignity to put on pants drop off their kids, go home to clean, work, cook, and eventually repeat the cycle. Maybe as I age, the anxiety will die down. Maybe not. Either way, I find talking about the realities of raising noisy kids with a noisy mind gives me hope. It makes me know that I am not alone in the daily struggles and gives me the strength to forge forward.

I DON'T NEED YOUR SHIT, SUSAN. I'M ALREADY HARD ON MYSELF.

Each and every day we get up. We drink our coffee and we tackle the world. We get our kids ready for school. We pack lunches, drive the minivans to school drop-off, head to work or back home, and do our best to survive, and at times enjoy the day.

During the process of this we fail . . . a lot. We fail dozens of times. We forget to switch the laundry for the eighth time and now have to rewash it because it smells like mildew. We fail by forgetting to sign permission slips for field trips. We fail because life is hard and having kids is exhausting, and did I say life is hard?

Each day we encounter people who make those failures even harder. The Susans of the world try to get under our skin as they deliver backhanded compliments and straight-up insults to our in-boxes. Sometimes, when they are feeling brave, they even say it to our faces. This piece is directed at all the Susans.

Ten Things You Should Never Say to Any Mom at Any Time

1. You look so tired. Is your baby keeping you up all night? Mine has been sleeping through the night forever. You should sleep-train.

2. I bet you could totally lose that baby weight if you went full "keto" and ordered my shakes and joined my online exercise group. You could look so much better.

3. You should probably look into medicating your child. He might be on the spectrum. I have a friend whose child is "special." I can have her call you.

4. You look stressed. You should try to get organized. Your life would be less of a mess if you got on a schedule.

5. You missed sign-ups for the class party. I took the liberty of signing you up for a home-baked item that is sugarless, flourless, organic, and gluten-free.

6. It's so funny running into you here. I haven't seen you in the gym in weeks. I assumed you had given up.

7. I think it is great that you don't overschedule your kids. I mean, my kids are so busy with learning Mandarin, the flute, sign language, karate, feeding the homeless, and soccer practice. It is refreshing that you guys don't force them to be great.

8. WOW, you pack Lunchables in your kids' lunch boxes? They must love having the "cool" mom who doesn't care about their nutritional needs.

9. Looks like you are hitting that dry shampoo pretty hard. I don't think it is a daily-use kind of thing, but I could be wrong.

10. It must be so freeing to let your child wear a Halloween costume to the grocery store in June. You are just writing your own little rule book, aren't you?

You are the one who takes care of your kids. You are the one who gets up in the middle of the night for feedings, diaper changes, and stomach bugs. You are the one your children look for when they are scared of the dark or when they are super nervous at an awards ceremony at school. They love you, and guess what? You do get to write the rule book. Every mom is supposed to be different, feel different, and parent different. We all have different kids who need different things. It would be amazing if we as moms could let other moms parent the way they see fit. What would happen if we could bite our tongues and let well enough alone when it comes to motherhood?

EXPECTATION VERSUS REALITY IN MOTHERHOOD

Motherhood is the hardest job you can't quit. The day they hand you that baby is the day you realize that your heart will now walk outside of your body forever. You are now in charge of a tiny human who will fight you tooth and nail on every subject ever discussed in perpetuity. It's anxiety-inducing for sure.

I recently realized that my expectations of certain situations were all wrong. I was expecting way too much out of myself when it came to motherhood. I needed to set the bar lower—way lower. I needed to evaluate expectations versus reality in terms of motherhood.

1. Laundry

The expectation is that I will be able to finish the laundry.

The reality is that it will never, ever, ever, ever, ever, ever be done. As soon as I finish what I believe to be the last load for the day, I will find a sock, or someone will piss the bed. Laundry never ends. So let's sunny-side-up this situation. If the laundry ends, it probably means I'm dead, so I guess it is good news that I have laundry to do.

2. Dinnertime with the family

The expectation is that we will all sit together and talk about what happened during our day. We will chat about school, work, and exciting social topics, and eat a delicious home-cooked meal.

The reality is that the majority of the people you cooked for will not like your food, which was probably burnt. When asked what they did at school today, the kids will all reply, "Nothing." Social topics will most likely include bugs, poop, and farts. Then, you get to clean up the mess and do all the dishes.

3. Teaching valuable life lessons

The expectation is that as parents, we know it is our duty to teach valuable life lessons to our children. When serious topics arise, we will quietly and calmly discuss the situation so that we can have an educational and deep discussion and learn the appropriate lesson.

The reality is that you will be in the grocery store one day and your child will see an individual who has no hair and your child will then point and loudly say, "Where did all of that man's hair go? Why is his head so shiny?" You will then have to quickly explain why it is rude to point and hope the bald man is cool with being bald, and then try to figure out why people go bald, or at least explain to your child that you can both sit down when you get home and ask Alexa why people go bald.

4. Bath Time

The expectation is that you will sit in the bathroom and enjoy tubby time with your children. They will laugh and play with their tub toys, and you will bond and have wonderful memories of bubble-bath tubby time.

The reality is that all children think bath time is an excuse to work on their 50-meter freestyle Olympic trials breaststroke. Working hard to be the next Michael Phelps, however, they will exit the bathtub wet but not clean, as they did not actually complete the purpose of the bath, which was to use soap and shampoo on their stinky bodies.

5. Bedtime

The expectation is that you will snuggle up with your children and read them a delightful bedtime tale. You will hold your beautiful blessings in your arms and create lasting memories of rhyme time with Dr. Seuss and watch them drift off to sleep.

The reality is that you will read them a bedtime story and they will demand another one. They will then tell you that they need a glass of water. You will finally get them tucked in and once your butt hits the sofa cushions, they will be screaming for you, with their heads peeking through the cracked door, like Jack Torrance from *The Shining*. This cycle will repeat for many, many moons. Eventually one of you will end up crying.

The lines between expectations and reality can get very blurry. It can be so hard to remind ourselves that what we see online and in the movies is not what we will deal with in our homes on a daily basis. None of this is easy; however, all of it is worth it. Lowering the bar has allowed me to retain some of my sanity. I implore you to do the same.

YOU'VE RUINED MY LIFE: AND OTHER STUFF OUR KIDS SAY TO US TO TRY TO KILL US

Do you remember how much you wanted your child to say his first words? You would look at him and say, "Say *Momma*. Say *Momma*. Please, honey, say *Momma*!" You wanted to hear this bundle of joy that you have cared for, loved on, fed, changed dirty diapers for, and woke up for in the middle of the night to cuddle and soothe show his love for you with a simple word, *Momma*. Now, 14 years and two additional kids later, I am praying they would "PLEASE STOP TALKING FOR TWO MINUTES!"

What's my point? Motherhood is a complete and utter contradiction. We love our children so damn much, yet they annoy the piss out of us on a daily basis. However, as a mom, we are programmed to think that we can't admit that our little blessing is annoying us to the point of no return. I absolutely have unconditional love for my children even though they can be straight-up assholes. Sometimes it seems that they say things just to hurt us. Could that be possible?

Have you ever been brushing your daughter's hair and she begins to squeal and scream about the exact height and location of the ponytail you are attempting to complete? You are struggling to loop the hair tie around one more time without breaking it, and she is pulling away from you and whining about how tight it is?? Anyone? Anyone? And then she looks in the mirror and says, "That's not what I asked for! I asked for a low ponytail. I'll do it myself!" And you watch her pull the ponytail out and walk away? That child was absolutely trying to give me a heart attack. Listen, kid, I just spent ten minutes doing YOUR hair. Cut the crap and be happy with your ponytail.

Our kids know just how to bring us to our breaking point. They drive us to the edge and poke and prod and push, until we are teetering. Some of my own children's examples of the poke, prod, push . . .

1. Mom, this dinner tastes disgusting.

2. Mom, your butt jiggles like Jell-O.

3. Mom, you never spend any time with me. Why don't you love me?

4. Mom, stop it! You are so embarrassing.

5. Mom, you never let me have a hamster.

6. Mom, you never go swimming with us.

7. Mom, you have a bald spot.

8. Mom, you have hairs on your chin.

9. Mom, you smell like onions.

10. Mom, I have a school project that was due yesterday but I forgot to tell you about it, and now I need a working volcano by tomorrow.

There are so many parenting books out there, yet there truly is no road map for this journey. It's pretty funny when you think about it. My kids can't drive. They don't have jobs; therefore, they have no money. They rely on me for their ultimate survival, yet they think I have no idea what I'm doing, and they tell me how much I am ruining their lives on a daily basis. If we are being honest, I don't have any clue as to what I'm doing, but I've been doing it way longer than they have, so there's that.

Any time I get in the car to take the kids to school or practice, or run errands, at least one kid tells me that I'm going the wrong way. How the hell do they know where I'm going, and how on God's green earth do they know it's the wrong way? "Mom, this isn't the way to Target. Did you forget where we are going?" Seriously, kid? You think I don't know where Target is? FOR. THE. LOVE! Every time they do this I can feel my blood pressure rising. Mind your business, kid, I've got this. Not that it's any of your business, but we have to go to a few more places and then Target. "I don't want to go anywhere else! WHY DO WE HAVE TO DO THAT????" It's like they know how close I am to the edge, and they think, "One more push, that will do her in. I'm sure of it."

CHAPTER SEVEN

I Don't Want to Trade in My Perky Breasts: Aging Gracefully in a Filtered World

I am no longer 18. I have given birth to three children, and I gained 50 pounds each time. My body has been stretched to its limits. I have cellulite. I have gray hair. I like ice cream and wine. I make no apologies for my appearance. This is me. I am a hot mess. I like me. Guess what? You should like you too. Let's talk about aging gracefully in a world that loves to put a filter on every fucking picture we snap.

THE DAY I FOUND A GRAY HAIR ON MY DOWNSTAIRS PARTS

I started finding gray hairs at 25 years old. My mom had gone gray early, so I always assumed I would too. I dyed my hair, so it didn't really bother me. As I entered my 30s, the gray hair filled in more and I had to dye it more often. I was in the salon chair almost every six weeks. I am a relatively low-maintenance kind of gal, so this was torture for me.

By the time I hit 37, I quit dyeing my hair. I didn't want to worry about the upkeep. I actually didn't mind my silver streaks. I had earned each and every gray hair. I have been through a lot in my 40 years. Married at 23. Mom by 25. I have taught middle and high school. Diagnosed with an esophageal tumor at 34; realized that life is in fact really fucking short. Started a blog. Started a vlog. Started an online business. Became a comedian. Wrote a book. Evicted my uterus. Wrote a second book. Won an Oscar for best script writing for my dramedy. Wait—that hasn't happened yet. I'll keep you posted.

I am not sure why it never dawned on me that if the hair on my head was going gray, so would the hair on my hoo-ha, but the day finally arrived. In my 38th year on this planet, it happened. I was getting into the shower and I looked down. There it was . . . a gray hair on my lady bits. It was sticking straight out. It was loud and proud. My muffin had sprouted a gray hair. "Come here!" I shouted to my husband. "Come into the bathroom. I have to show you something." He ran into the bathroom and said, "What is going on? What's the problem?" I pointed at my landing strip and said, "It's going gray. My vahina is going gray!" He laughed out loud. "So what?" What did he mean, "so what?" My lady bits were officially old. This was life altering. I had so many thoughts racing through my mind.

1. Was it time to put my va-hina out to pasture?

2. Was my muffin now officially a "dusty" muffin?

3. Is it possible that your vagina ages the same way dogs age? So, if I'm 40, that would make my vagina 40 x 7 = 280 years old. That seems excessive. Maybe I am going down a rabbit hole.

4. Should I carry around a defibrillator in case my vagina flatlines? You never know when it might need a jump.

5. On the upside, perhaps my vagina ages like a fine wine.

6. Are there AARP benefits available for "silver snatches"?

7. I never took those Kegel exercises seriously. Can I start now or is it a lost cause?

8. Should I start using those yoni eggs? You know, the stone eggs you shove up your vagina to strengthen and tone. I'm afraid that as I am walking the aisles of the grocery store, they would fall out and crash on the floor of the cereal aisle. What if an employee picked them up to return them to me? I can't do this anymore. No yoni eggs for me.

9. Vaginal steaming has been all the rage. We can thank Gwyneth Paltrow for that. Perhaps a nice mungbean steam will do wonders for my gash. Wait, I just googled what V-steaming is and I have decided that it's a hard pass.

My husband then told me he was willing to help rejuvenate my old lady vagina with a regime of daily exercise. He says, "I have something for that."

After discussing all of this with my husband in the bathroom, we had a good giggle. It wasn't time to put my vagina in a nursing home. Our sex life was way better than it ever had been. For the first time ever, I was comfortable with my body. I was comfortable telling my husband what I wanted in bed. I was excited to try new things. On a side note, he has asked me to get a blond wig and dress up as I decided to go with #5 and believe that my kitty, like a good wine, gets better with age.

MY FIRST MAMMOGRAM

I had my first mammogram the year I turned 40. I found a lump in my right breast. Actually, my husband found the lump. We were in the middle of some sexy time and he stopped, mid-pump. I looked at him and asked what was wrong. He rolled over and said, "Is that a lump?" I moved my hand from his family jewels up to my breast. It did seem to be a lump. I told him not to freak out and suggested we get back to the business at hand. We somehow got back into the swing of things and finished up our sexy time.

But when we got into the shower, I did a breast self-exam. I have very tiny boobies, so lumps are pretty easily detected. I have always been a bit lumpy, but this lump seemed to be sizable. I made an appointment for the following week. My husband joined me for the appointment and we both agreed that it would be a good time to have my first mammogram.

I was taken back and told to undress from the waist up. I put on the super sexy smock top, the kind that opens in the front, and impatiently waited for the technician to take me into the exam room. She finally arrived after what seemed like an hour, and walked me over to the machine I lovingly named "the Boob Smasher 3000." She explained that it would only take a few minutes to complete the scans. She asked me to open up the smock and place my right breast into the machine.

I began to laugh, as my breasts aren't big enough to be "placed" anywhere. I got as close to the machine as humanly possible and leaned in. The technician looked at her screen and walked back over to me and said, "Nope, we need more." More? I had no more. I am a true-blue A cup. Maybe even a negative A cup, if that is a thing. I still buy my bras in the junior section of the department store.

She pulled on my boob like taffy and began to smoosh my breast down with the top of the machine. All I could hear in my head was the song "Push It" from Salt-N-Pepa, although in my head it sounded more like, "Ah, smoosh it, smoosh it good."

We did this "smoosh it" dance for five more minutes. She smooshed and pulled, and at one point, I think she cracked one of my ribs. It wasn't her fault; I wasn't offering much to work with. My tiny ta-tas resemble flat pancakes with cock-eyed nipples, courtesy of breastfeeding three babies who ate like ravenous wolves.

When we were done, she showed me the scans and said, "This should be enough." I wasn't sold, but she was the professional. The next eight days were the longest in my life, but I finally heard back from the imaging center and was given the all clear. My lumpy breasts were full of fibrocystic tissue and cysts, but nothing to be concerned about. The moral of the story is to be vigilant and do breast self-exams. Big or little, lumps happen. Do breast self-exams each and every month.

I SURE HOPE FAKE TITS SAG

If there is any justice in the world, fake tits will sag. Why would I say such a thing? I guess because I always wanted a nice pair of boobies and I never got them. When I was 15, my mom joked that the "boobie fairy" must have missed me. Now at 40, gravity is pulling my tiny deflated pancake breasts toward my belly button.

So yeah, I want to know that gravity affects us all equally, regardless of surgical intervention. Don't get me wrong, I'm good with where I'm at, but watching a sex scene in a movie and staring directly at a set of beautiful, perky fake breasts kind of makes me snarly, and I want to know that justice—in the form of gravity taking its toll—will one day be served.

I'd also like to see her ass sag and a muffin top appear, but for now I'll take seeing her fake tits sag. I also really want her name to be Susan.

THIS IS JUST MY FACE

Being a wife and mother and running a business is exhausting. What's the expression, "rode hard and put away wet"? Apparently that means to look haggard. However, if we are being honest, I haven't been wet without the assistance of K-Y Jelly in several years. Thanks, perimenopause! Back to my point. I am one of those people who wear their tired on their face. Some days it's a badge of honor; others it is simply terrifying to walk into the bathroom and catch a glimpse of my face in the mirror. My brain is telling me I'm around 25, but my mirror is clearly screaming, "This is 40!"

A few years back, I was at the gas station. I had just dropped the kids off at school and I was in my Mom uniform, black yoga pants and a stained T-shirt. I opened my car door and trash fell on the ground. I bent over to pick it up and I heard a voice behind me say, "Hello." I turned around and saw a middle-aged man at the pump beside me. He was putting gas into his pickup truck. I gave a polite nod and continued to throw out the trash that I had asked my kids to throw away six months ago. I opened my gas hole, or whatever it's called, and put the gas nozzle in. I leaned back on my minivan and retreated into the vast abyss that was my exhausted mind.

The gentleman continued to attempt small talk with me and I did my best to nod. Finally he looked at me and said, "You should try smiling sometime." I'm pretty sure every woman who reads this has had a similar experience. This jackass who knows nothing about me just told me I should try smiling. My look of annoyance and disdain must have been apparent because he continued by saying, "I just think you would be in a better mood if you smiled. You look a bit angry. I'm sure you're pretty when you smile."

Why do men feel the need to tell women to smile? What does my face have to do with your world? If I wanted to smile, I would damn well smile. Believe me, I love to laugh. I spend tons of time doing that. I also love to smile when my kids tell the punch line of the joke first, or when my dog greets me at my front door. I know how to smile and I do so as I see fit. It is no one's job to tell anyone else what their face should look like. I'm proud of every wrinkle, every line, every memory that I wear on my face.

If we are being honest, I wasn't angry at that moment; this is simply what my face looks like. This is the face of years of up-all-nights. This is the face of a morning struggle with an autistic son who didn't want to wear pants to school today. This is the face of packing three school lunches. This is the face of 75 knock-knock jokes before 7 A.M. This is simply my face. It's not an angry face. It's not an unhappy face. It's not the face of a mother who wants to run away, although the thought has crossed my mind. Once again, this is simply my face.

I would love to go back to that gas station and tell that man how much I love my face. The day he told me to smile, I didn't have the words I needed to express that. I gave him another nod and continued to look off into the abyss, thinking about how I wanted to throat-punch him and every other person who told me over the course of my life that I would be prettier if I smiled. As I age, gracefully or otherwise, I have learned a lot about myself. I am no longer sorry for shit I shouldn't be sorry for. I will not smile for others. I own who I am and who I want to be. I do not owe anyone anything. I am a motherfucking force to be reckoned with. This face is perfectly imperfect. Spending time trying to conform to the perception of others is not my responsibility and I refuse to take part in it. Let your face be yours. Let your face tell your story.

LEAN INTO LOVING YOU

When I was in my early 20s, I was super critical of my body. I was never satisfied with my looks. I wanted to be thinner and tighter, and I wanted breast implants. Now that I'm 40, I have to laugh. I wasn't able to appreciate my body back then. I think part of that was because I didn't really know who I was. I was insecure and lacked confidence.

Over the past 13 years, my body has drastically changed. I have had three children and five surgeries. My nipples have been eviscerated by breastfeeding. My tummy looks a bit Frankensteinish. I have cellulite and stretch marks.

I used to hate when my husband would squeeze my waist or thighs while we were in bed together. I would cringe if he wanted to leave the lights on. I was so afraid of my imperfections being seen. My body was not the body you see in magazines or in porno flicks. I assumed those were the bodies my husband wanted.

While I was getting ready for church one morning, I looked in the mirror and saw a sea of gray in my hair. I thought, "I've earned this. I'm okay with this." I'm so happy that I am now able to embrace those imperfections and welcome these changes.

As women, I think it is very important that we own our bodies. We need to own our personalities too. If you are loud, be loud. If you snort when you laugh, SNORT! We need to own our choices. I have failed at many things over the past six years with my businesses. However, failing means I am actively trying. I own each of my failures just as proudly as my successes. I have learned to love myself. No one can truly love you if you do not love yourself. As a result of loving myself, my relationship with my husband is stronger. We are now in year 17 of our marriage. None of it was easy, but all of it has been worth it. My relationship with my children is stronger. My kids know that I hustle my ass off. They know that if I am leaving, it is because I am working. They know that I have goals and dreams to chase. They also know that while I am gone, I miss them terribly. I don't think I will ever get used to sleeping under a roof without my kids. It's actually the thing I dread most about being an empty nester.

I am able to take risks simply because I can. Every risk I have taken for my business or family has been stressful. However, I have the ability to take those risks. I GET to take those risks. I positioned myself to jump. Guess what . . . so can you!

You can learn to love yourself. You can learn to find happiness. That might mean getting therapy. It might mean talking to your spouse or another family member. Maybe your pastor at church. The hardest part of this journey for me was realizing that I had to take an active role in figuring out what made me happy. I spent most of my life making sure everyone else was happy, and I avoided doing things to make myself happy. If you are struggling, please know that you are not alone. Your insecurities do not need to rule your life. You are enough. You are beautiful. Your imperfections make you amazing. They make you strong. They make you courageous and unstoppable.

The best thing I ever did for myself was find myself. If you are lost, I promise you are still in there. Keep searching. Take the time to listen to the voice in your head and give yourself the benefit of the doubt. You are enough. You are beautiful. You are perfectly imperfect.

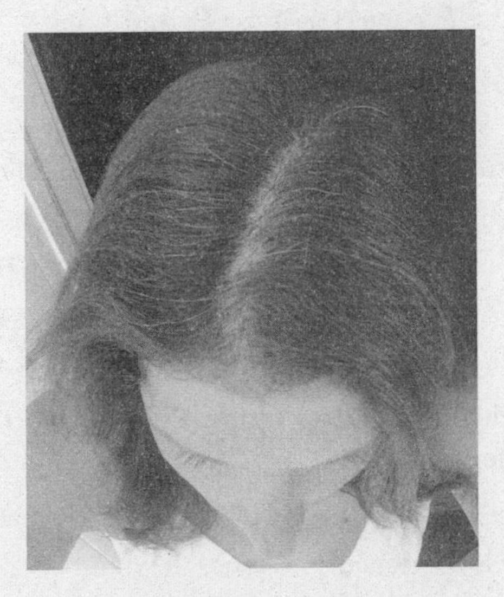

YOU'RE BEING DISRESPECTFUL TO THE CHAMBER OF COMMERCE

I love speaking engagements. I have spoken at women's empowerment conferences. I have been asked to tell jokes as a warm-up act for events. I have traveled across the country and met so many amazing women. I truly love speaking about my why. You know, the "why" I do what I do. Last year I was asked to speak at a Women in Business event for the Brooksville Chamber of Commerce. Brooksville is a small town in Florida, about two hours from where I live. The morning of the event, I was getting dressed in the hotel while the kids ate breakfast. I was wearing a pair of jeans, a T-shirt (one of the T-shirts in my online store), and my trusty Converse sneakers. My hair was in a bun and I went the extra mile to put on some mascara and a nude lipstick. We piled everyone into the minivan and I put the location of the event center into my phone.

My husband started the minivan and looked over at me and said, "Are you going to change your clothes before we get there?" I said, "What? I'm ready." He said, "You can't show up like that—you're being disrespectful to the Chamber of Commerce." I quickly took a look at what I was wearing and for a split second I thought to myself, "Oh shit. What have I done? I don't have anything else to wear; this is all I brought." I paused for a minute, and then I got super pissed. Like really, really fucking pissed. I said, "How am I being disrespectful? This is who I am." He continued by saying, "It would have been nice if you dressed up a bit. This is a business event." I did my very, very best to remain calm. I said, "I understand that. I have been running this business for five years. I am my brand. I am speaking to a group of women who run businesses. They asked me to speak. They are getting me. Not a different version of me. Not a dressed-up version of me. They are getting me."

I started to sweat, which isn't odd for me; also it was June in Florida. I felt my face flush. I was not going to be told that my brand was disrespectful. I know everything there is to know about my brand. I created it. I live it. My husband looked at me and remained quiet for a few minutes. He finally said, "I'm sorry. I didn't look at it from that perspective." I accepted his apology and collected my belongings and said good-bye. I got out of the car and walked into the event center.

I was taken upstairs to get ready for my keynote speech. The room began to fill with women from all walks of business. Some were in dresses. Some were in slacks. I was introduced, and in that moment, I knew I had to open my speech with the interaction I'd just had with my husband. After telling the story, I explained how I was upset with myself for thinking I had made a mistake. For a split second, I'd listened to what someone else thought and I was doubting myself. In that moment, I was doubting my brand. I was doubting my business. I was doubting who I was to my core. I allowed my husband to cloud my judgment. I knew exactly who I was and the message I wanted to pass on to these women. I purposely avoided dress pants or a skirt, because I don't wear that shit. I am a leggings- or jeans-wearing woman who loves to design

T-shirts. If nothing else, I am true to who I am, and it is so damn important to hold tight to that. I love my husband, but I am the only expert at being me.

As women, wives, mothers, employees, and business owners, we tend to doubt ourselves and listen to what others have to say about how we should do things. How we should raise our children. How we should run our businesses. How we should navigate our marriages. I am not saying that we don't need help or advice at times, but I cannot doubt who I am or what my brand is. I am my brand and I sure as shit know what that means. It means that I wear jeans, T-shirts, and Converse to speak at events. It means that I am unapologetic when it comes to knowing who I am and where I want to go with my business. It means that I have zero fucks to give and I will own my failures and my successes. It is absolutely freeing to truly know who you are. It has taken me a long time to get here, and I have no intention of going back. Don't apologize for who you are, or for trying to figure out who you want to be.

CHAPTER EIGHT

You Are a Motherhood Expert: I'm Not Kidding

I am a mom to three amazing children. I know when they are sad. I know when they are happy. I know when they are faking a sibling-induced injury. I know them better than anyone else knows them. That is my job. I am an expert when it comes to Matias, Brian, and Sophia. That doesn't mean I won't get it wrong from time to time. It doesn't mean they will always agree with how I handle situations with their friends or their punishments. It means that I am enough. I am exactly what they need. It is not my job to be the world's best mom. It is my job to be the best mom I can to them, and no one else. Don't try to be something you're not; that isn't what your children need. They need the mom who was chosen for them, you. You truly are the best mom . . . no engraved coffee cup needed.

PARENTING EXPERTS AND THEIR PERFECT PARENTING ADVICE

I fly often, and I have never been tempted to give a pilot advice on how to fly a plane. I have had five surgeries in the past four years, and not once have I contemplated giving my surgeon advice. What I'm getting at is, these professionals are considered experts in their fields. I have no business telling a pilot how to land a plane, and don't get me started at attempting to cut a person open with a scalpel—I have a hard time pulling my own kids' teeth. If we can respect that professionals are better at their jobs than we (people who know nothing about their jobs), why do people offer unsolicited parenting advice so often?

Not too long ago, I had a parenting expert write to me to explain that I am a disgusting parent who is trying her best to ruin her children's lives. He continued on to tell me that if I read his research, there was a chance I and my children could be saved. He told me all about his credentials, how he is an expert in the parenting field and has over 20 years in the educational field. I messaged him back and told him I was happy to read his works. I really was, as I love to see what everyone has to say about everything. I do not claim to know it all.

He sent me a few links that I read through. After I was finished reading, I asked him how many kids he had and their ages. I also asked him how his methods worked on his children. A few minutes later, he replied that he does not actually have any children but he has thoroughly done his research.

I am sure he read tons of books and I am sure he has done tons of research, but parenting is a contact sport. To become an expert at parenting you need to get dirty and live in the trenches. You need to do the up-all-nights and the diaper changes; you need to listen to the hour-long crying episodes. You need to experience firsthand the wrath of a toddler in Target who is not going to get the toy that she so desperately wants. YOU HAVE TO EXPERIENCE IT! There is no book on any shelf out there that can fully prepare you for what parenting is going to be like. I have read so many books on parenting, but some of the best advice I have ever gotten has come from other parents in my parenting circle.

I once read that you need to practice something for 10,000 hours before you can be an expert at it. That sounds like a long time, but it's actually only 1.14 years. I have been parenting for over 122,640 hours. I would wager that I am somewhat of an expert at parenting my own children. Did you read that? I would consider myself an expert at parenting my OWN children, not your children, not the neighbor's kids, and not the kid at the bus stop who is always picking his nose. My kids are my business, and your kids are yours. End of story. And to every parenting expert who isn't a parent, stop it. Come back to me 10,000 hours after you have children of your own.

20 WAYS YOU ARE AN EXPERT AND DIDN'T EVEN KNOW IT

Guess what?!?!? You are a parenting expert too! Here are 20 ways you are a certified parenting expert, and not just simply certifiable.

1. You can determine which kid farted by scent alone. If you only have one kid right now, hang tight. I promise you will be able to hone this skill. I guess we can call it a skill.

2. You know which foods make your kids super hyper, and yet you still let them have it on their birthday, special occasions, or Halloween.

3. You know your child's favorite song forward and backward. You also let her listen to it on repeat in the car—that is, until you actively feel your brain explode. Then, it's time to switch it up.

4. You know what time to cut your child's water intake prior to bed to avoid bed-wetting accidents.

5. You lie awake at night and dissect your every move, thinking about ways you could have handled a situation better, so you can be better the next time. This is a big one. Like a really big one. The fact that you care enough to do this means so damn much!

6. You know your kid's favorite meal. You've cooked it a million times, even if you don't like it.

7. You bring cupcakes to the PTA bake sale. They might not be homemade, but you remembered. Or, like me, you got to the school and had forgotten the cupcakes, but went back to the store to buy some, and then went all the way back to the school to drop them off. Whew!

8. You ask your children how their day was, each and every day, fully knowing they are most likely going to tell you they didn't do anything at school.

9. You can tell the second your kid is getting sick. Like the first sneeze. "What's wrong? Are you feeling flush? Does your throat hurt?" You are on it like Dr. Mom, and your kids always want to snuggle in your lap when they are sick. They will also be sure to sneeze directly in your open eye, because love.

10. You also know when your child is faking it. Really, kid, that is the worst fake cough ever. Then you ask why he is trying to avoid going to school. Most likely a test or an assignment. You then take the time to stop and talk to him about his anxiety.

11. You are constantly thinking about your children, even when you don't want to think about your children. BOOM! This one happens more frequently than

I had ever anticipated before having children. There is no off switch for this.

12. You feed them. Like every damn day. Every damn meal. I don't think I knew how much kids ate before having them.

13. You house them. Yup, rent-free.

14. You cart their asses all over town. Practices, school events, movies, out with friends, anywhere they need to go. You get them there!

15. You tell them you love them, even when they have been complete ass-hats that day, or week, for that matter.

16. You support their adventures, even if those adventures cause you to lose sleep and make you worry about them. Yup, there is that worry component again.

17. You know when your child is lying. Each kid has a tell. You become a poker queen!

18. You call your children out when they are lying, because you want them to grow up to be moral and kind people.

19. You hold them accountable when they make the wrong choices. Even when they "hate" you for it. This one can be a doozy, but it is so fucking important.

20. You get up each and every day and you do it all over again. PREACH!!!!!!!!

You, my friend, are a parenting expert! You know your children better than anyone else on the planet. Go with your gut. Do what you think is best. I am all for asking other parents for advice or tips, but in the end, you've got this. You know what needs to be done, even when it can be so very hard to do.

I AM NOT MY CHILDREN'S FRIEND; HERE'S WHY

Friends are people you can relate to. You have gone through similar circumstances; you can see their point of view. A friend is someone who could potentially pick you up from the airport. (This would have to be a really good friend, because no one wants to go to the damn airport.) Friends will offer advice at times, while remaining silent at other times when they know you just need to vent. Friendship is a wonderful thing. At no point in the past 14 years of raising children have I thought of my children as friends.

My children rely on me. They need me to feed them, put a roof over their heads, offer them guidance, and at times (depending on the age, sometimes WAY more often than not) they need me to lay down the law. Yup, they need me to whip their asses into shape. They need me to be an authority figure in their lives. I truly believe that all humans need boundaries and structure. We need to know where the lines are. It can be so difficult to navigate when we have no idea what is expected of us.

I am not my children's friend. I am the mom. I am the one who loves them more than they can imagine. I am the one who birthed them. I want and need them to know that they are special and loved, but they are not my peers. They have no idea what it's like to be me, and they shouldn't. I don't need them at this age to really understand how unfair life is. Part of my job is to shelter them. I work really hard at finding the balance (I hate that fucking word. *Balance* means you keep it all and do it all. That is impossible. You have to give things up.) between being too hard or too soft on them.

My children can call me at any hour of the day or night to pick them up. They can come to me for advice. They can ask me anything, but as their parent, I will not be giving advice as though I am a friend. I will be giving advice as a mom. Those things are completely different. When I give advice to a friend, I know that my friend is an adult. I know my friend has the experience necessary to formulate an educated opinion, based on many factors. My children do not. My children need me to guide them, and at times, take them by the hand.

It can be really hard to keep the lines clear and distinct. At times, you may want to gossip with your daughter about the mean girls in her class. You might want to tell her that girls like that will never have her back, and that she shouldn't attend those sleepovers because mean girls can cause a lot of drama. However, your daughter needs to learn that on her own. Your daughter needs to know that the friends she chooses will provide advantages and consequences. She will need to experience that, so she can decide how to handle gossip and rumors. Your daughter needs you to guide her; she doesn't need you to roast a ten-year-old, no matter how much you want to—and you WILL want to, I promise.

My children are still young, but I hope one day, when they are grown, we will be the best of friends. I hope that they will say, "Mom, now I understand why you yelled about the laundry and the toys." Because they will have children of their own. We can sip coffee and gossip about whoever the hell they want to trash-talk. I truly believe that is a rite of passage, and I am really looking forward to it. I want to be best friends with my adult children, so I need to be the best mom for them now.

FINDING YOUR PARENTING WINS WHEN ALL YOU SEE ARE FAILURES

A lot of parenting is boring. Hear me out. Every single day I do laundry, dishes, parent pickup and drop-off. I pick up toys, flush toilets that my delightful blessing forgot to flush, and yell, "PUT ON PANTS!" Parenting can be a very monotonous cycle. With that being said, that cycle can cause you to see all of your parenting failures and none of your wins. Which can be very, very hard.

Sometimes I like to lie in bed at the end of the day and remind myself of my wins. It might seem silly, but sometimes I need to find a win. Some days are utter shit storms, and I really, REALLY need a win. How about a "for example." Mornings can be tough. Getting three kids out of the house on time is basically the equivalent of performing a miracle. One morning, my daughter and I got into a fight. I started yelling, she started yelling, and by the time things had calmed down, I realized we were late. I rushed all the kids out of the house without feeding my daughter breakfast. The boys had eaten, but because my daughter and I were fighting, she didn't eat anything. As I pulled up to the drop-off line, I reached into my purse and grabbed a granola bar. I gave her the bar and said, "I love you. Eat this." She took the granola bar and placed it on the seat and then exited the minivan. She shunned my breakfast peace offering and went about her day. I felt awful after drop-off, and I parked my car and cried for about ten minutes. That night I was thinking about the fight, and I realized there was a parenting win in there. I'd told her I loved her and offered her breakfast. She didn't take it, but it was offered. I did my part. I had a granola bar in my purse for this exact situation, and I did my best. Sometimes winning is just about trying. It is just about being there.

My point is simple. Parenting wins come in all shapes and sizes. Each day we will win. Each day we will lose. However, every day that we get up and grind, we can go to bed knowing we made a difference. We were present. We were involved. We showed love.

I ABSOLUTELY TREAT MY KIDS DIFFERENTLY. HERE'S WHY.

Anytime I hear someone say, "I treat all my kids the same," I wonder how that is possible. With three kids, two boys and a girl, there is no way I could treat my kids the same. My children are all very different. It really does amaze me how different they can be, considering they all came from the same gene pool.

My oldest is very sensitive and quiet. He has a tendency to quit things once he feels like he has mastered them. My middle child, my daughter, is a lot like me. Hard candy shell, gooey soft inside. She loves to be the center of attention. She is loud and beautiful. My younger son is a comedian. He is very black-and-white. He is smart and could probably outrun the Energizer bunny.

Sometimes I think we forget that our children are people. What I mean by that is that these tiny humans are actually going to grow up someday and live in the real world without us caring for them. They have personalities and quirks. They have likes and dislikes. They are all different and unique. So how on earth can we treat our children the same?

A lot of parenting is learning how to motivate our children to get them to do things that we need them to do. We have to motivate them to do their homework. We have to motivate them to do their chores. We have to motivate them to practice hard at their sports and activities. I have found that what motivates one of my children will not motivate the others. I also do not punish my children in the same manner. Taking away electronics for one is not the same as taking it away from the others. My daughter is big into gymnastics. If her grades slip or she or acts out, I take away the gym. That really gets her attention. However, my oldest really isn't into sports. So, when he was playing flag football, telling him he would miss practice if he acted out probably would have been a blessing for him.

I am not going to worry about treating my kids the same. I believe that would be a huge disservice to the adults they are going to grow up to be. My kids are different, but I love them equally. (That might be a lie. I love the one who sleeps the longest the most. I'm kidding . . . kinda.)

KEEP YOUR SICK KIDS HOME FROM SCHOOL: AKA DON'T BE AN ASSHOLE

I taught for 13 years in the public school system. I spent the first three years with a chronic sore throat and runny nose, due to all the germs these kids passed around. It is bound to happen. Kids get sick. It is part of building immunity, and the school system is a cesspool for germs. It would always irritate me when a student would come to school with a fever or rash. However, once I had kids of my own, it infuriated me. I understand how hard it is to miss work and take a sick day to stay home with your kid, but come on! Why on earth would you send a kid to school with a fever, pinkeye, head lice, or hand, foot, and mouth virus??? I totally understand that things can go undetected at times, but one year we had such a massive outbreak that the day care had to shut down for professional biohazard cleaning. Parents kept sending their kids into school with the hand, foot, and mouth virus. My poor kid ended up getting it three times over the course of six months.

One year there was an outbreak of rotavirus. If you don't know what rotavirus is, you are lucky. It is the most intense stomach flu you can get, and the smells. OH MY GAWD, THE SMELLS. The only thing that can rival the smell of rotavirus diarrhea is most likely the phosphorus depths of hell.

When you have multiple children, you will experience any virus they pick up in a time-lapse sequence. It usually goes like this: Kid one comes home from school sick. You immediately triage the situation. You now have roughly 24 to 36 hours before kid two will most likely get sick. Once symptoms from kid two emerge, kid three will go down in the same 24-to-36-hour window. You will then spend the rest of your time attempting to wash your hands and sanitize every surface of your home. You will then spend about two hours cleaning out your AC ductwork and spraying two to three cans of Lysol into the air return until your home smells like the ICU of an award-winning surgical center.

When people send their kids to school sick, they are spreading those germs to literally everyone. The teachers, the janitors, the front office staff, and all of their family members. It is never fun to have sick kids at home, but think about all of the students and faculty members who have compromised immune systems. If you send your kids to school sick, and one of their classmates brings home that virus to Grandma, who is fighting cancer, it can be deadly. I know this sounds super dramatic, but I lost a friend who was battling cancer because she picked up a secondary infection from a day care.

Wash your hands. Teach your kids to wash their hands. When your kids are sick, keep their asses home. When you are sick, keep your ass at home. And if you really want to have a heated debate, listen up! Go get a fucking flu shot. That's right, I said it! Flu shots are here to protect us. They are here to protect the young and old. They are here to help fend off a virus that kills people each and every year. And while we're at it, make sure to vaccinate your kids at their well visits. Yup! I went there. Vaccines are so important to our global health. I have a child with autism, and there is no research that points to the fact that a vaccine gave my child autism. So do us all a favor and don't be an asshole. Keep your sick kids home from school.

STOP ENABLING! YOU NEED TO LET YOUR KID STRUGGLE.

We are living in an era of lawn-mower parents who bulldoze every obstacle in their kids' path. We are currently raising a generation of kids who do not know how to make their own doctors' appointments or pay bills. Yes, we have a boatload of entitled brats running loose in society disguised as adults. It is scarier than any *Friday the 13th* film I have ever seen. Why is this happening? you might ask. Well, it's pretty simple. Parents don't want their kids to struggle. They want to make sure that their children will succeed and have a better life than they did. They want them to have all their hopes and dreams come true. While all of that sounds wonderful, it is a very dangerous path.

Struggle is an important part of life. We all need to struggle in order to learn what's important. We all need to fail in order to learn how to succeed. My older son was taking an online algebra class last summer. He is an average math student, so I was a bit worried that an online class might be tough for him, but he was required to take it. We set up a schedule for him to work on the class each day, and my husband would check his online scores at the end of the week. I would remind him to make sure he was keeping up with his studies, but I was not on top of him like a helicopter. He was in eighth grade, quickly approaching high school, so he needed to be responsible for his assignments.

He was nearing the end of the course and was working on the semester review. He came to me after dinner and said, "I failed the review. What am I supposed to do?" I said, "Well, if you failed, you will need to go back, study, take notes, and do it all over again." He began to beg and plead with me to call his teacher to ask if the grade could be forgiven and if he could just take the test. This child had lost his damn mind. There was no way in hell I was going to call his teacher and ask him to forgive an assignment that he had failed. I got my husband and made my son show his father his review sheet. My husband is great at math, while I can't perform a math problem if it involves division or letters. He took one look at the review and said, "Go back to chapter one, page one, and retake your notes. Once you have new notes for the entire semester, you can redo the review, and once you pass, you can take the test." My son began to cry. He hated that math class and didn't want to redo the review. He went into his room, surely cursing his father and me under his breath. He then spent the next four weeks taking notes and doing study sessions with the teacher. He eventually passed the algebra class with a B, but it was a struggle. We fought. I yelled. My husband yelled. My son cried. He begged. He wanted a life preserver, but the real life preserver was when my husband told him to go back and DO THE ACTUAL WORK! Our children need to struggle to find ways to save themselves. They need to feel that struggle so they can work the problems and create solutions. If we take it upon ourselves to fix everything for our kids, they will barely survive life and never truly thrive. Take the time to allow your children to struggle now, so in the future they will reap true success, and move the fuck out of your house because they have a good job.

I REFUSE TO SET UP COLLEGE SAVINGS ACCOUNTS FOR MY KIDS, AND THAT DOESN'T MAKE ME A BAD PARENT

I was on a live feed one day, talking about my kids, and I mentioned that I do not believe in paying for my kids' college. My parents didn't pay for me to go to college, and not every kid should go to college. Well, I got some death threats after that live feed. I was called everything under the sun. I was ill equipped to be a mother and my kids should be taken by Child Protective Services. I was a monster. I'm not sure why this topic struck such a chord, but it didn't change my mind. I still feel the exact same way.

College is not for every child. There are thousands of careers that do not require a college degree. We have an entire service industry that needs workers. My mechanic makes a killing and he never went to college. He drives a nicer car than I do, and I know he's an avid golfer, so I assume he is doing well financially.

Also, I am still paying off my student loan debt, and guess what? I AM NOT USING MY COLLEGE DEGREE. I am writing this book about inappropriate thoughts I have on motherhood, and my college degree is in History, early colonial America to be exact. I don't want my kids to be saddled with student loan debt, so they'd better save up, get a job, or get a scholarship. They'd better want to go to college and be serious about college. If they aren't, then they should pick up a trade, become a cashier, or pursue a passion that does not require a four-year degree.

COLLEGE IS NOT FOR EVERYONE. I firmly believe that we force kids to go to college because we think that is the best and most successful plan and path for them to be on. My baby brother hated school. He graduated at 19 and got into the AC trade. He began working as a technician and then worked his way up to sales manager. He now owns a house, a boat, and a big hillbilly truck, and has ZERO student loan debt.

My point is very simple. I do not believe in forcing my kids down a path that might not be right for them. If they choose to go to college, they'd better be serious about it. They'd better work hard and apply themselves. College is very expensive. If they want to work in a field that does not require a college degree, they'd better learn that trade inside and out. They'd better work so hard that the boss notices them and wants to promote them because of their amazing work ethic. I will not love my children more or less based on their decision about college. Life is way too damn short for that.

CHAPTER NINE

Different-Needs Parenting in 2020

My youngest son has autism. Autism is not who he is, yet it is part of him, and at times it can be all-consuming. Brian suffered a brain injury at birth and was later diagnosed on the autism spectrum. I have learned so much by being Brian's mom. I am so lucky he is mine. I needed to learn the many lessons that being his mom have taught me.

I use the term "different needs" because I truly believe that all of my children are "special" and they all have "different" needs. Being a different-needs mom can be exhausting, overwhelming, mind-numbing, and joyous, all at the same time. If you have a child with different needs, please know you are not alone. I know you feel alone, but there are so many moms out there who are learning to put the pieces of their child's puzzle together.

THE DAY MY PEDIATRICIAN SAID, "HE MIGHT HAVE CEREBRAL PALSY"

Brian is my baby. He is ten years old now, but when he was 15 months old I took him to the pediatrician because I was concerned. Brian wasn't walking. Brian wasn't talking. Brian was a happy baby, but he wasn't doing things my other two children had done by this point. My husband and I each had our own concerns, but we were simply hoping that Brian would catch up and things would be just fine. I will never forget the day our world changed.

We went into the doctor's office. The wall had a mural of the solar system. There was Saturn; I know that one because of the rings. Earth, that was a given, and I probably knew the other planets as well, but I was too busy worrying about what the doctor was going to say to remember all the details of the black and blue-gray mural that pulled me into orbit that day. I sat there with Brian in my lap. He was such a happy baby. He wasn't walking yet, so I carried him everywhere. He was literally attached to my hip.

When the doctor came in, he asked me to put Brian down so he could see him stand. I put him on the floor and he stood there on his tiptoes, like he always did. He held on to my hand and just looked up at me, waiting for me to pick him up. His knees were all callused because he crawled everywhere, and it was obviously time for him to start walking. The doctor began asking tons of questions. Questions about my labor and delivery. Questions about Brian's diet. Questions about Brian's legs and feet. He examined him and then put him back down on the floor.

He looked at my husband and me and said, "It could be a million things, but I need you to be prepared. Your son might have cerebral palsy." Once those words came out of his mouth, my brain shut down. I don't remember the rest of what he said that day, but I knew what cerebral palsy was. I knew it meant that my son might have brain damage. I knew that in that moment I was not able to process any of this.

We were instructed to see an orthopedist and a pediatric neurologist. Brian would need X-rays, MRIs, and CAT scans. We spent the next several months in various doctors' offices, and I personally spent those months blaming myself for whatever was wrong with my son.

Two orthopedists agreed with our pediatrician. They told us that Brian's bones were normal and healthy. He should and could walk based on the physical structure of his bones. We then went to a neurologist, who ran several tests and scans. It was the week before Thanksgiving. I was exhausted and overwhelmed. They told us we would get a call the following week. They said to enjoy our holiday. I replied that we would, fully knowing I was going to worry about this every minute until we had some results.

I was standing at the sink washing dishes on the morning of Thanksgiving when the phone rang. It was the radiologist from the MRI center. They called to let us know that Brian was perfectly normal. His brain was fine. No evidence of CP. My heart was so excited but then sank. Why couldn't he walk if his brain and his bones were fine? I attempted to celebrate with my husband and enjoy the day. It was great news. I needed to be happy about it. But the news didn't settle with me.

The following Monday the phone rang again. It was the neurologist. He called to let us know that the radiologist who called us read the wrong report. Brian did have brain damage caused by a birth injury, and he did in fact have cerebral palsy. I began to cry. Some of the tears were sad, and some of the tears were happy. We finally knew what was wrong, and now it was time to figure things out.

We met with the doctor the following week and he explained that Brian would have some motor skills issues. He would need leg braces. He would most likely have some learning disabilities, and was at a much higher risk for being on the autism spectrum. The portion of his brain that was damaged also makes potty training difficult and can cause incontinence, the inability to hold urine, for the duration of his life. Basically, Brian might never be fully potty trained.

The doctor told me that Brian would struggle, but he would be able to do almost everything, if not all the things "normal" kids can do. I would need to let him struggle, mentally and physically, but he would be able to figure things out.

Brian wore leg braces for a few years. He was diagnosed with autism at the age of four. He started playing soccer at the age of five. He was placed in the accelerated program at school at age seven. He still isn't fully potty trained. He wets the bed several nights a week. We are hoping as he gets older that he will be able to manage this, but if not, it's just pee.

Brian's diagnosis was one of the scariest things I have dealt with as a mother. I know how lonely it is. I know how isolating it is. I know how much guilt you carry when your child is diagnosed with something. You want to take the blame and wear it like a scarlet letter. You want to fix your child. I also want you to know that it will be tough to navigate those waters, but you don't have to do it alone. Talk to your family. Talk to your doctors. Talk to your spouse. Support will get you through to the other side.

ANGER AND RAGE IN THE FORM OF A TINY CHILD

The kids were having a good time playing outside. That is, until my oldest said something that set off my youngest. Brian has issues controlling his anger and rage. He hits. He screams. He melts down. He can go from all smiles to fury in a matter of seconds. We have been working on how he reacts and how he is the one who has control of his actions. It can be so hard for my other two children to understand what is going on when he is in the middle of a rage fit. They don't want to see him hit me. They don't want to see him lash out.

Learning how to control your reactions is hard enough when your brain is wired correctly. My son's brain damage complicates things. We have the same conversations over and over again. We work to give him outlets for his anger. We work to make sure he learns to self-soothe. We work to give him space and let him know that he will be able to figure this out. We work with a behavioral therapist. We go through our breathing techniques. We talk about where our rage and anger stems from.

He gets exhausted. We get exhausted. It's a completely different type of tired. I call it bone tired. After these meltdowns take place, I have him nap or at least try to find some quiet. I usually sneak back in after a few minutes to make sure he is okay. I do this because I need to see that the rage has left his body. I need to know that he has been able to find himself again. I know how awful it feels to be full of rage. I hate that feeling. I want to make sure that he starts to feel like himself again. He is not his rage.

He is not his poor choices. He is not his anger. Those are emotions and it is okay to feel them. I am doing my best to help him work through them. It is not easy. There are days when he melts down once. There are days when he melts down five times. There are days when he and I are both so tired we feel like a shell of ourselves. But at the end of the day, I know he is not his autism. He is not his brain damage. He is not his rage. He will learn to cope and deal because we will be there to help him along the way. To every parent out there who is helping their children find their way, I applaud you. This journey is exhausting, but it's worth it.

AN OPEN LETTER TO MY PERFECTLY IMPERFECT SON

I wrote this letter a few days after Brian's diagnosis. He was 4 and I was 34. Writing this letter was one of the most therapeutic things I had ever done for myself. I urge you to write letters to your children. It gave me a chance to vent and make peace with some of my raw emotions. I needed to get these things out of my mind and try to make sense of them. As parents, we are learning as much as our children each and every day. The second I think I have something figured out, a wrench is thrown into the mix. Life simply happens. Take some time to write letters to your children, and when you are ready to give the letters to them, they will be so grateful that you did.

To my son,

I love you. You get to be the baby forever. We knew the day that you were born that something was different about you. The doctor was late and I was told to wait. We waited a bit too long. We didn't know it for the first year, but your tiny brain went a while without oxygen. It caused some brain damage and we still aren't sure exactly what that means. The cerebral palsy caused your left leg and arm to move a little different from the right side, but they get the job done. I can see how smart you are; there is no hiding that. It might take you longer to solve the problem, but I know you can do it. You amaze me every single day.

You are one of the funniest people I know, and I'm pretty funny if I do say so myself. You make me laugh each and every day. Your knock-knock jokes are the best. Your laugh is infectious. I also cry almost every day. I cry because it isn't fair. I cry because I lose my temper. I cry because I am exhausted. I cry because I just want you to be "normal." I cry because you don't sleep, and I need you to sleep. I cry because you still aren't potty trained and you are the only kid in your class that wears a diaper at nap time. I cry because my heart hurts for you.

This past week I took you to the doctor and they confirmed that you also have autism. Just like I knew that something wasn't right before, I knew that this was also a possibility. It didn't make it any easier to hear. I cried when I took you home from the doctor's office. You asked me what was wrong. I didn't reply.

I know that you are exactly who you were meant to be. I cry because I don't always know how to help you. I cry because I can't find the patience to give you exactly what you need. I cry because I fear that you are broken and I don't know how to fix you. I cry because life is hard enough when you are "normal."

I know that you are happy most of the time. I know that you love me all of the time. Please know that I love you too. I love you even when I am sad, and even when I cry. I love you when I yell and when I say things like, "I am on my last nerve." I will do whatever I can for you, no matter what that looks like.

You have a beautiful soul. I try very hard to remember that when you are kicking and screaming. When we are in public and I have to leave the store or the restaurant because the meltdown is a level 10. I cry when you hit me, or your brother or sister. When you scream and cry and I just can't figure out what set you off. I try. I promise you that I will always try.

You are not your brain damage. You are not your autism. You are my son. You are a comedian. You are a boy full of energy and ideas. You are my shadow. I love every piece of you. I cannot fix you because you are not broken. You are a puzzle that was put together with a different method. It's my job to care for you and love you just the way you are. Perfectly imperfect, just like the rest of us.

Love, Mom

20 THOUGHTS THAT ENTER THE MIND OF A DIFFERENT-NEEDS MOM

I have three kids. All of my kids make me wonder things. My youngest is autistic, and more often than not, my thoughts go to a very different place because of his different needs. I try hard to find the humor and silver linings in our daily trials, but sometimes it just sucks. Autism sucks.

Every parent struggles. Sometimes I think we parents of different-needs children have different thoughts that travel through our minds. I think most parents blame themselves for things that happen to their children. When you have a child with different needs, however, it gets even easier to play the blame game. When my son was first flagged as developmentally delayed, I blamed myself. I thought back to the few drinks I had when we went out on a date night before I found out I was pregnant. I thought about the foods I ate while pregnant. I thought about how I was shocked when I found out that I was pregnant, thinking I was done having babies, and not sure if I could handle one more. Did my thoughts of uncertainty do this to my baby? I had all of these thoughts and so many more.

1. Did I do something to make him this way?

2. Why does every day have to be so tough?

3. Will this ever get any easier?

4. Who doesn't like socks? They are made of the softest cotton, yet he shrieks when I put them on him.

5. Who doesn't like underwear? I mean, we are all supposed to wear underwear, right?

6. Maybe the diagnosis is wrong.

7. Maybe someone can fix him.

8. I need him to sleep. He never sleeps, and I am so tired.

9. I can try that new diet I read about and take all the food dyes out, but that seems like a lot of work. I wonder if it would be worth it.

10. It is hard enough to worry about a kid with no issues; this is freaking exhausting.

11. Go ahead and stare at my kid as he screams in the store. You have no idea what our life is like.

12. Will he get married?

13. Will he always need me?

14. What happens when I'm gone?

15. He is hilarious. I wonder if he knows how funny he is.

16. How did I get so lucky to get this little dude?

17. I couldn't love him any more; he fills up my heart.

18. They keep talking about medicating my son; maybe they should medicate me.

19. Tomorrow is a new day.

20. You can't fix what isn't broken. So I guess I will keep doing what I'm doing and know that he was made exactly the way he was supposed to be.

Being a parent is the most difficult job on the planet. Parenting is tough no matter what. However, being a parent to a child with different needs takes the game to a different playing field. Each day brings new surprises and trials. Each day brings disaster and hope. Each day is a good day, because we are still alive to enjoy it.

I am sure that most of you have had some of these same thoughts about your children, even if they don't have different needs. The journey is different for all of us, and magically a lot of it is the same. It is a fantastic feeling when parents can relate to each other. It is so nice to know that we aren't alone.

TEN THINGS "SPECIAL NEEDS" MOMS WANT YOU TO KNOW

Kids are kids. Whether they are "normal" or "special needs," they all need the same things. They need love, affection, attention, structure, and a parent who puts them first. Sometimes I have a hard time explaining what it's like to have a child who is on the spectrum.

Here are ten things I want my mom friends to know.

1. I'm exhausted: Anyone who has kids knows what exhaustion is. My son is autistic and has OCD. In the morning, we have to go through a very specific routine or he becomes agitated and cannot get ready for school. Some days when I leave the house, I feel like I have already had an eight-hour day.

2. I didn't forget you: Sometimes I get swallowed up by my world. I forget that there are other people out there. I am not trying to be a bad friend. I am not trying to be neglectful. I am simply trying to survive.

3. It's not a fit, it's a MELTDOWN: I have been at the grocery store and had to leave due to an F-7 meltdown. My middle child used to throw fits in the store; what my younger son does is not a fit. A fit can be contained or controlled in a short period of time. My son's meltdowns have lasted for hours. I have had to leave stores, doctors' appointments, and restaurants. When my son has a meltdown, he cannot control what he is saying or doing.

4. Don't be sorry: Being supportive and being sorry are two totally different things. I am not sorry that my son was made differently; you definitely do not need to be sorry. My son is a blessing. He is hilarious. He is my hero. I never feel sorry for him, and I don't feel sorry for myself either.

5. I will talk when I am ready: If you ask me how things are going with my son, I may or may not want to talk about it. When my son was diagnosed, I didn't tell anyone for about a week, not even my family. I knew he had various issues, but hearing the words "Your son is autistic" was very hard. Sometimes I want to vent and rant and rave; other times I don't want to utter a word.

6. I'm green with envy: I am not a fan of the word *jealous*, but sometimes I am very jealous of "normal" families. I see how easy it can be to pick up and go places without all of the chaos. I forget that my family is the exact type of normal that they are supposed to be.

7. I need a girls' night out: If you plan a night out, invite me. I need to go out. I want to go out. If I make an excuse, call me on it. It is important and healthy to get away from the kids and the mess.

8. Share your advice: I love to hear advice. I think that it takes a village to raise children. Give me your tips and tricks, and I am happy to share mine as well. Remember that what works for one of us may not work for the other, but special-needs children are no different in that respect.

9. Don't say "I know": If you don't know something, it's okay to admit it. If I am telling you a story about getting my son dressed and how it took me an hour to put on his socks and shoes, and you have never experienced that before, don't say, "I know." Say, "That sucks." Say, "I'm sorry your morning was so hectic." Say, "Wanna have a drink tonight?"

10. We have the same job: Don't look at me and think I am doing a different job. The end goal is the same. We want to produce good, honest, moral, happy human beings. We may need to take different paths to get there, but the destination is the same.

Knowing is half the battle. If you have a friend who is a special-needs mom, love her, support her, listen to her, and be there for her.

THE BLUE PLATE THAT BROKE US

I was struggling. Like really, really, really struggling. We had been going to the behaviorist with my son for about six weeks and we had hit a wall.

We had bought books, we were trying new behavioral interventions, and we were working hard to understand.

The problem was, I really didn't understand. I wanted to, but I didn't.

Autism is like a maze. One of those crazy, scary-ass corn mazes out in Iowa where every turn brings some new unwanted adventure. You know what I'm talking about. Like in the movie *Children of the Corn.* Freaky scarecrows and demonic children with sickles, popping out from around the corner to give you a heart attack—and at times succeeding. I didn't understand why my son had such a hard time listening. I didn't understand why he got so mad so quickly. I didn't understand why he had to hit and punch and pull hair. I didn't understand why he couldn't sit still. I didn't understand why he wouldn't sleep.

I wanted to understand, but right then I just didn't. I felt like because I didn't understand, it made me a bad mom. A mom who cared less. A mom who couldn't give my son what he needed. I wanted to give him what he needed, but sometimes I couldn't.

This frustration I had was MINE and I understood that, but I wasn't sure what to do with it. When I was working with him to "establish the desired outcome," I wanted to say, "Why the hell can't you just do what I asked you to do?" I didn't want to be super patient and calm. I knew I had to, but it is very difficult to do.

That morning, the tipping point was the blue plate.

MOM: Do you want waffles?

SON: Yes. Can I have syrup?

MOM: Sure. Please sit at the table.

SON: (*Walks into kitchen*) I want them on a blue plate.

MOM: I already put them on a paper plate so I don't have to clean it.

SON: I want a blue plate.

MOM: Today we will eat waffles on this plate.

SON: (*Throws body to the floor and begins to scream*) I said I want a blue plate!

MOM: Do you want waffles?

SON: YES!

MOM: Here are your waffles—please take them to the table.

SON: NO! I want them on a blue plate. Put them on a blue plate. Why aren't you putting them on a blue plate!

MOM: (*I cannot do this anymore. I need to get everyone else breakfast. This has now eaten up ten minutes of my time. I put the waffles on a blue plate.*) Here, go to the table.

SON: (*Picks up waffles and syrup gets on hands*) I can't eat these now; my hands are sticky.

That led to a fit that lasted over an hour. He went to his "safe spot," which was my closet, and cried and threw shoes. He came out screaming four or five times. We did the routine about six times before he came out calm.

It wasn't even noon and I was exhausted. I just wished he could understand that the blue plate could be any plate. He didn't need the blue plate to be happy. But I guess in his case he did.

So, I cried over the blue plate. Autism sucks. I don't want to travel the maze today.

WILL I SURVIVE THE TEENAGE YEARS OF AUTISM?

At ten, Brian is now on the edge of puberty. He is a smelly boy who loves to run around like a greyhound on a track, chasing that rabbit like it's his damn job. He is full of energy. Like, so full that he wakes up several times a night because the spark plugs in his brain are always firing.

I have been navigating the waters of autism for ten years now. TEN. I know it isn't a long time, but it feels like a long time. It feels like I have been running a ten-year marathon, where I got a break to sleep once a week, and then I had to start all over again.

I was standing in my kitchen the other day looking at Brian. He is getting taller. He is getting stronger. The kid can do ten pull-ups in a row and already has a chiseled six-pack of abs. It's a bit intimidating. As I was looking at him, it hit me. He is going to go through puberty soon, and puberty is a bitch. Like a really awful, skanky bitch that slashes your car tires and keys your car doors. Puberty has run rampant through my house like wildfire over the past three years, and I am now actively worried about dealing with Brian and his autism as he experiences it.

His emotions are all over the place. I am not sure how I will handle his fits of rage. I have no idea how different him going through puberty will be from the way it was with my other two children. I don't even want to think about having the sex talk with him right now, or what it will be like when he wants to date. Right now, if you ask him what he wants to do when he grows up, he will tell you that he wants to live in a shed in our backyard. He wants a dog, but not a wife. He told my husband and me that wives talk too much and he doesn't want to upset his dog.

However, one day that will change. One day a girl will catch his eye, and he will be flooded with hormones that he can't control. One day he will want to impress that girl and prove his love. I hope that he will be able to control those emotions as he makes his way through puberty. The hormones run so hot, and he is already my tiny rage monster. I am worried that more testosterone will flood the system and we will have to run for the hills.

So I am doing what most moms who have kids on the spectrum do: I spend time online, researching things like "Will I survive puberty with my autistic son?" and "Tips on how to save my liver during the puberty."

CHAPTER TEN

Who Knew Being a Mom Was So Damn Lonely?

When my husband and I had our first child, back in 2006, I had no idea how lonely it would be. I assumed that once you had a baby, you would automatically be in love with that tiny person, and colors would look brighter, sounds would be sweeter, and life would magically make sense. I was so, SO very wrong. I did fall head over heels in love with my son, but I was also immediately isolated and overwhelmed by becoming a mom. I think it is so important to discuss the transition to becoming a mom, as well as how that journey changes and shapes us. THERE IS ABSOLUTELY NO ROAD MAP TO RAISING CHILDREN. Yes, there are tons of parenting books, but parenting does not have a recipe. There is no guarantee that if you follow the instructions, you will end up with award-winning blueberry muffins—I mean healthy, well-adjusted children. You get what I'm saying. If you are feeling alone and isolated, ironically, you are in good company. Let's talk all about it, shall we?

I'M THE MOM

I'm the mom; I have to be happy. I can't let anyone know that I struggle at times. I'm not supposed to complain or vent. I need to keep it all in at all times. I need to be the rock. I need to be the beacon of light, whatever the fuck that means.

I'm the mom; I can't be afraid. I need to smile and pretend that life is just fine. If I show the world that I am cracking, the truth will come to light. Everyone will know I am ill equipped. Everyone will know that being a mom doesn't come easy to me. My mask will fall and I will be cast as the imposter. I have to keep smiling, even though it is the last thing I want to do right now. Like, literally. I want to smile less than I want to do laundry.

I'm the mom; I have to get it all done. There's so much to do and never enough time. The list never ends. It doesn't end when I am asleep. It actually robs me of peace and quiet. The list dances in my head and plays leapfrog with my sanity.

I'm the mom; I have to enjoy this. I'm told all the time how much I'll miss this. Why am I going to miss this? I mean, who really misses changing dirty diapers and washing mountains of laundry? I'm not a fan of only owning furniture that is covered in maple syrup. I know I'll miss my kids' tiny hands and feet. I'll miss their toothless smiles. But can we agree we won't miss everything? Please!

I'm the mom; I'm so very tired. Tired when I wake, tired when I try to fall asleep. I'm actually tired of being tired. I know the kids will get bigger and I will find more time for sleep and hobbies, although I don't remember what hobbies are. I just wish I could get some of that sleep now. I feel like sleeping now would be amazing.

I'm the mom; I have to be strong. I can't let anyone know that at times I feel like I might break. Not just break, but completely shatter. Like into a million tiny pieces. Pieces that no amount of Gorilla Glue could put back together. Pieces that I would have to sweep up off the floor, and then mop. So I try not to break, because I know I will undoubtedly have to clean that mess up as well.

I'm the mom; everyone needs me. I have to be available at all times to everyone. Which is so fucking hard and confusing, because I am simply one person. Just the one.

I'm the mom; the weight I feel is so heavy. At times, it's so much that I feel it in my bones. I worry that my bones will be crushed under the weight. Turned into dust. Which, once again, I would have to clean up. Luckily, I have a Dyson vacuum and that sucker is intense.

I'm the mom; can anyone hear me? I speak, but it seems that my words are silent. I yell. I scream. I beg my children to listen.

I'm the mom; I love them so much it hurts. Am I screwing them up? Do they know how much I love them? Like, I would kill for these tiny assholes. I would sell every single thing I own for them. Mind you, most of it is broken, stained, and unusable, but the sentiment is the same. I would do anything for them. They are my heart.

I'm the mom; why am I so lonely? These feelings I feel are exhausting at times. I think it's safe to say that most moms have felt this way. I think we've all struggled a bit. I think it is so important to discuss our mental well-being and the stigma that is associated with talking about the struggles of motherhood, the raw, real side that people don't want to talk about. Because that is where most moms live.

We need to talk about what life is really like when you're the mom. Life without filters. I am not ashamed to be a hot mess of a mom. I am not ashamed to share my daily fears and struggles. I want you to share as well. You are not alone. Talk about your fears. Talk about the hard parts of motherhood. Talk about all of it. Reach out to your friends and family and let them know how you are feeling.

MOM GUILT IS REAL AND IT'S PAINFUL AF

It is funny how emotions elicit physical reactions. I mean, I know that's what's supposed to happen, but I was truly not ready to deal with the physical reaction to mom guilt. I had/have mom guilt frequently. I think most moms do.

I was determined to breastfeed with my first child. I didn't really give it much thought prior to delivery, I just knew I wanted to breastfeed. Fast-forward to the day he was born. What a clusterfuck that was! I am not sure if everyone's first delivery is so awful, but mine sure was. I had no idea what to expect, even though I read *What to Expect When You're*

Expecting. I wanted to have a natural birth, so I refused pain medication when I got to the hospital. BIG MISTAKE. My contractions were getting closer and closer together. I was writhing in pain. I called the nurse and told her I'd changed my mind. It's amazing how pain can quickly get us to undo nine months of planning. She checked my cervix and said, "I'm sorry, sweetie. You are too far. We are actually going to get you ready to push." The look on my face must have said it all. I angry-screamed, "I'm sorry, what did you say? I said I changed my mind. I want the epidural." Well, that ship had sailed.

They began to prep me to push. I did everything the book talked about. I tried to find my focal point on the wall so I could do my breathing. My husband attempted to calm me down. My sister was down by my foot, looking like she was staring at a car wreck. My sister was 12 at the time. I told her she didn't want to be in the room, but she begged me to let her stay. I think she might regret that choice now. She still doesn't have kids. Back to whatever the hell I was saying.

Things went sideways quickly. My son got stuck and they had to use the vacuum, twice. Eventually he entered this world with a very egg-shaped, beautiful head. He was so perfect. So beautiful. Such a gift. The nurse handed me my son and I felt no pain in that moment. I was flooded with emotions. They took him to clean him up and I lay there with my poor, tired vagina, still in my doctor's hands. He was stitching me up. I had been cut from one hole to the other. It was messy and so very painful. My poor husband had a look on his face like, "You asshole! You broke my fucking wife's vagina." I didn't want to look at it ever again.

My son came back from his bath and I was told to feed him. I took him and put him to my breast. He tried to latch on, but nothing was coming out. They assured me that he was getting something. I kept doing that on and off every hour. My milk really hadn't come in, and his crying intensified.

We did that dance for about seven days. I would try to breastfeed, he would try to nurse, but neither of us could figure it out. I was becoming more and more distressed. My breasts hurt so bad from my milk coming in. He would latch but then get flooded with milk and choke. I was miserable and crying. He was miserable, crying, and hungry. It was so damn hard. I was ready to throw in the towel. My husband was out golfing with friends and he called me. "Hey. So I think I have something to help you breastfeed. I will stop at the store on my way home and get it for you." I thought, "Seriously, this asshole thinks he can solve this breastfeeding thing? What a dick!"

That night, he came home with a Medela nipple shield. If you don't know what that is, it is a thin piece of plastic that you pop onto your nipple that helps the baby latch. He handed me the plastic nipple and said, "My buddy that I was golfing with said his wife used this when she had trouble breastfeeding." I opened it up and washed it. I read the package and figured, what can I lose? I popped that plastic nipple onto my actual nipple and I prayed. My son latched on and started going to town. It was like he had been left in the desert for a week and I finally decided to offer him a drink.

I started to cry. I was so overwhelmed with joy. I was carrying so much mom guilt for my inability to breastfeed. I had only been a mom for a week, but I felt as though I had already failed as a mother. No one ever told me how hard it was to breastfeed. I assumed that it was easy and natural for everyone. It wasn't. It was one of the hardest things I have ever done in my life.

The guilt was so powerful. I'd felt like I was unable to provide for my child. That guilt tore me to shreds. That guilt fed me lies. That guilt caused me physical torment. Mom guilt is real and we deal with it on a daily basis. I think if we talk about the experiences that cause us mom guilt, we can learn from each other and learn how to deal with this awful monster. This was my first case of mom guilt, over 14 years ago. I have danced with that beast on many, many more occasions. I have also learned that it is a required part of the parenting journey. Why, shit happens. We will miss activities, tournaments, class trips, and life will go on. We feel that guilt because we are humans. But more than that, we are fan-fucking-tastic mothers!

THE EXISTENTIAL CRISIS THAT WAS ACTUALLY A QUEST

By the time I was 33, I realized that something was missing in my life. I had been a wife for ten years. I had been a mom for eight years. I started to become depressed. I was working full time. Life was a constant grind and I felt like I was unable to get off the assembly line. The worst part was that I felt guilty for feeling depressed. I loved my family, but I knew something was missing. I wasn't passionate about my job, and I had a massive void that needed to be filled. After I put the kids to bed, I sat in the bathroom or in my closet and cried. Often. If my husband found me, he'd ask why I was crying, but I didn't have an answer.

I woke up in the morning in a zombie state. I struggled to get the kids off to school. I talked myself into getting ready for work. I packed lunches, checked backpacks, planned Crock-Pot meals, and wished I were somewhere else. Yes, that's right. I wished I were somewhere other than my kitchen, listening to my children fight over the last pack of fruit snacks. I dreamt about a life that was less stressful and more enjoyable. These thoughts made me cry on the way to drop my kids off at school. These thoughts made me feel like I was the worst mother on the planet. These thoughts made me feel like a terrible person.

Anxiety and depression are paralyzing. I felt awful, but I didn't know why. I wanted to feel better. I wanted to be happy. I wanted to have passion and fire in my soul. I began to think, "What is wrong with me? Why do I feel this way? What am I doing wrong? Everyone else is happy. Everyone else is living a great life. It's me. I am the problem."

Every time I logged on to Facebook and saw families out at the park, or on vacation, or posting a perfect family picture, I winced in secret shame. Why was everyone else happy? Why were all of these people so put together, so on top of things, so amazing? How did they afford to go on vacation every other week? How did they keep up with work and life and managing to cook every meal from all locally sourced, organically grown products while milking a goat in their backyard? What the hell was I doing wrong? I rarely posted anything on Facebook. My kids were always running around. I rarely had on pants when I was at home. The dinners I prepared were constant Pinterest fails, and I didn't want anyone to know I was struggling. Really, really struggling. I was a mess.

On the surface, I was managing to keep it together for the most part. I was able to take care of the kids, get myself to work, do all of my wifely duties. I was surviving. I was alive. However, I was not living.

I remember going for a run in May of 2014. I remember the exact street corner I was on when I had a very scary thought. I said to myself, "What if this is it? What if this is all my life is supposed to be? Am I okay with this?" I wanted to un-think it. It made me nervous and uncomfortable to have even had the thought. My life was a great life. My kids were healthy, my husband was loving and faithful and had a paid-in-full life insurance policy to boot. I didn't have my dream job, but I had a roof over my head and a full belly. Why was I having these thoughts? Why was I such a selfish asshole?

What kind of monster dreams for more when she has all of this? I couldn't un-think the thought. It just hung in the air. It stayed with me. I had finally let the secret poop out of the dark, scary corner of my brain, and I acknowledged its existence. I was a monster. I was my own problem. I had spent the last ten years claiming to be a selfless person. I was in fact a very selfish person who was only pretending. I was pretending to be the happy wife and mother. I was pretending to be someone who had it all together. I was pretending to live.

Now I had a problem. What was I supposed to do to fix it? I sat down and started to think about the things I love to do. I love to tell stories. I love to talk to people. I love to laugh. I wasn't embracing any of that in my version of "living."

This is the part where you might think, "This lady is crazy. She is such a selfish asshole. She has everything she needs and yet she wants more." And you would be absolutely entitled to your opinion. I *was* being selfish. I *was* thinking of myself. I hadn't put myself first in ten years. I'd let my dreams wither away. I gave every ounce of my being to my husband and my children and I let the secret poop pile up and fill the dark corners of my mind. I put everyone else first because as women, as mothers, we are told that we must take care of everyone else before we can take care of ourselves. By doing that, I lost myself. I lost my way. I lost my path.

By putting everyone else first, I was hurting myself and my family. I was not the best mom. I was not the best wife. I was not the best me. I was a Mom-bot who was in survival mode, simply going through the motions.

I needed to find my passion. I needed to live my life. I was simply surviving, and surviving wasn't enough anymore. I wanted more. Admitting to myself that I needed something else was incredibly scary. It went against everything I was taught. Why was I revolting? Why couldn't I just let well enough alone? Why did I need more? What was I searching for? Why couldn't I just be happy?

I'd played this game of hide-and-seek for years. I assumed it was best for everyone if I just kept it to myself. But by keeping it in, I was not only hurting myself, I was hurting my marriage and my children. As moms, we need to know who we are as humans. Being a mom is part of who I am; it is not the entirety of my being. I LOVE being a mom. However, it is one part of me. It has shaped me and changed me for the better, but I am still in here. Luckily, that tumor that we discussed earlier gave me the push I needed to pursue my passions. It gave me the courage and strength to truly understand that life is way too damn short. That tumor saved me. That tumor helped me find myself.

Motherhood has a way of taking over every single inch of us, and that can cause an identity crisis. I am so grateful for the existential crisis I discussed above, paired with one of the scariest situations I have ever dealt with in my life. It forced me to start writing and to create a community where moms could discuss the real, raw realities of motherhood and marriage. That crisis was in fact a quest. I think all women have to go on a quest after becoming moms. It is simply part of the journey.

Do you feel better knowing that another mom questioned everything about her life? I hope so. I used to think I was the only one who had ever felt that way. Now I know that these feelings are normal and a part of this parenting journey. We can fight it or we can embrace it. I have gone back and forth between both of those places, and I can tell you that embracing it, learning how to roll with it, leaning into parenting and who you are as a person, is a truly beautiful thing.

CHAPTER ELEVEN

It's Just a Phase . . . Son of a Bitch! The Whole Thing Is a String of Phases!!!

Sometimes as parents we lie to other parents, not on purpose necessarily, but it happens. I was talking with my cousin Eric, whose toddler, Mason, was in the middle of his "terrible twos" phase. As a typical toddler, he would cry to get his way, say "No" repeatedly, throw himself to the floor, and turn into a limp noodle when you went to pick him up. All normal toddler stuff. I attempted to reassure Eric that this was just a phase, and it too shall pass, when it hit me. Raising children is simply a string of phases. Why had no one told me that? Well, I am here to let you know, raising kids is simply a string of phases. As soon as you feel like you have your feet planted firmly on the ground, someone will pull the rug from under you. It goes that way for everyone, so don't feel too special.

NEWBORNS MAKE YOU REALIZE YOU DON'T ACTUALLY NEED SLEEP TO SURVIVE

I love to take naps. I was always a person who could sleep in. Before I had kids, I loved weekends because I liked getting up and starting my day at 10 A.M. I had a very rude, very early awakening once I had my first child. FOR. THE. LOVE. The first few weeks were a complete blur. Days blended into evenings, and evenings blended into some form of what I can imagine an acid-induced psychotropic high would look like. It was the first time in my life that I was truly sleep deprived.

It really is amazing how long we can last without proper sleep. I mean, it isn't healthy or easy to do, but it is possible. My firstborn was a constant nurser. He was on my boob around the clock. I had no idea what I was doing in terms of breastfeeding. My doctor told me to feed him when he was hungry, so every time he cried I would stick him on my boob. We did this nonstop for the first six months. I was a complete disaster. I was so tired all the time. I was waking up every two hours to feed him. I looked and felt like shit. I was able to function, but I was a shell of my former self. Sleep is so important for our mental health and physical well-being.

I was at a well visit with my baby and he started to cry. I began to nurse him and the doctor asked me how I was doing. I began to cry. I started talking about how tired I was. How I felt like a cow hooked up to a milking machine. I talked about how it was hard to function during the day. She asked me why I wasn't sleeping. I let out an audible laugh. I said, "I am up every two hours feeding him. The baby is always crying, and the only things that makes him stop crying is feeding him." She looked at me and said, "He is six months old. He doesn't need to eat every two hours."

I felt awful. I was overfeeding him and screwing up his entire life. I'd managed to fuck this up in a matter of six months. At that point, the baby was done nursing. She took him and began to burp him. Right after that burp, he projectile vomited across the room. His vomit actually hit the wall, which was about eight feet away. She looked at me and asked, "Does he always vomit like that?" I said, "Yes. He spits up a ton and then gets really hungry again." I will never forget what she said next. "Oh my. Your son has acid reflux. This isn't normal. He is hungry all the time because he is throwing up all of his food right after he eats it. He needs to be on medication to help with his reflux."

I had no idea that this wasn't normal. It was my first baby. I assumed babies spit up, but I guess spit-up shouldn't hit the wall across the room with the force of a car crash—it was pretty powerful. "Will this medication help him keep his food down and sleep better?" She smiled. "Oh yes, this will help. You won't have to nurse as often and he will be much happier." I started to cry again at the thought of getting multiple hours of consecutive sleep.

We want sleep. We need sleep. However, much like the fairy tales we read to our children, sleep can be a fictional character that only visits us every once in a while. And somehow we manage to survive, and some of us even have more kids. Your body does what it needs to do and you chug along, just like the Little Engine who wanted to nap but never got to take a nap again.

TODDLERS ARE THE WORST

Toddlers. Toddlers are the worst. Toddlers only remain on our planet because they are unbelievably adorable. If toddlers weren't so damn cute, we would probably take a page out of the animal kingdom's book and eat our young. Yup, I said it. And guess what, I'm not sorry. Toddlers can be massive dickheads.

My daughter loves makeup. She is 11 years old now, but when she was an adorably awful toddler, she would go into my bathroom and play with my makeup. If you have a toddler, you know that silence is an extremely dangerous sound. I know as parents we all crave a little bit of quiet, but when you have toddlers, silence means that someone is fucking up some shit in another room.

I was in the middle of cooking dinner and it was horrifically quiet. I was boiling spaghetti noodles and just enjoying the sound of silence when it hit me. *Where are my kids and why is it so unbelievably quiet?* I started looking around the house. One was reading a book, one was playing a video game, and one was missing. I called my daughter's name. No reply. "SOPHIA! WHERE ARE YOU?" I started to panic a bit. *Did she get out of the house? How did I not hear the door open? How is it possible that I am such an awful mother? I lost my child while in my home. It's official: I am in fact the worst mother on the planet.* I kept searching the house, looking in closets and under beds. I opened my bathroom door to find my daughter covered in makeup and painting her nails. Nail polish was all over the floor and my makeup bag was covered with a bottle of liquid foundation.

Me: Sophia, did you open my makeup bag?

Sophia: No.

Me: Sophia, did you paint your nails?

Sophia: No.

Me: Sophia, you are wearing makeup and there is nail polish all over the floor. Are you lying to me?

Sophia: No.

That child lied straight to my face while wearing a full face of clown makeup. She didn't hesitate. She didn't blame it on someone else, she straight-up lied to me. Toddlers are the worst. But, like I said, she survived this because she was insanely adorable.

Toddlers are destructive. They are yearning for independence, yet they can't take care of themselves. They want constant attention, and at the same time, no attention at all. Toddlers are basically the equivalent of an independently wealthy 27-year-old trust fund child who never had to join adulthood, or the work force for that matter. On a side note, the nail polish never came off the floor. Every time I see the spot, it makes me think about the time she painted her face like Bozo the Clown and lied like a criminal in an interrogation room.

IT'S ELEMENTARY, MY DEAR. (THEME DAY, FIELD TRIPS, AGENDAS, OH MY!)

I remember the first day of kindergarten for each of my kids. It was exciting, liberating, and scary all at the same time. You are so excited to see them start a new chapter; however, you are worried about every single thing you could possibly worry about. I worry a lot, and I am a relatively creative individual, so my fears are rather descriptive and in turn cause me additional worry.

> ME: What if Matias falls in the bathroom and bangs his head? He could be unconscious and unable to call for

help. He will eventually dehydrate and become weak. No one will know he is in there in pain.

MY HUSBAND : This is the shit you worry about?

Eventually you get into the swing of things in elementary school. It was easier for me to send children numbers two and three, because, you know, been there, done that. However, having three kids in elementary school was rough. The only reason I ever get anything signed is because someone invented an app that my school now uses, so the teachers can send me messages. Without that app, I am not sure I would remember what school my kids go to. But between field trips, homework, agendas, theme days, lunch money, chorus, band, and after-school clubs, there is so much shit going on.

SOPHIA: It's crazy hair day.

ME: Okay.

SOPHIA: I need a dollar to participate and you need to make my hair crazy.

ME: Okay. (*I do her hair.*)

SOPHIA: This isn't crazy. This looks stupid. DO YOU WANT ME TO LOOK STUPID?

ME: Are you serious?

SOPHIA: Jessica's mom always does her hair right. You never do my hair right. UGHHHHHHHHH!

ME: *(Stares off into space, praying that my head doesn't explode all over the bathroom walls)*

SOPHIA: MOOOOOOOOOOOOOMMMMMMMM!

The elementary school phase is a fun phase. The kids are forming little personalities and making friends. However, it is hard to keep up. I swear, I think class projects were invented to test the stability of the parent–child relationship. I helped my daughter with a state facts class project once, and let me tell you, I don't ever want to go to Utah. Don't get me wrong, Utah looks like a beautiful place, but every time I think about Utah, I think about that class project and I physically become ill. (However, life is funny. We ended up going to Utah this past summer and it was gorgeous. My kids kept asking why there was a poop emoji on all of the speed limit signs. I had to remind them that Utah is the beehive state. It wasn't poop, it was a beehive.) Watching her type up her state facts, using one finger, one key at a time, while audibly sighing at how unfair it is to have to do a project, was painful. Almost as annoying as a yeast infection.

PUBERTY, TAKE ONE

Obviously, I survived puberty. I am a bit worried that at 40, I won't survive my children's puberty. OMG, THE ANGST!!!! My oldest is 14 and in the throes of puberty. My 11-year-old daughter has also begun experiencing "changes." FOR. THE. LOVE.

Having two kids going through puberty at the same time is like a BOGO special only Satan could conjure up. Sooooo moody. Sooooo full of emotions and hormones. I logically know that it isn't their fault that they are feeling and acting this way. Puberty takes your children and turns them into smelly, mouthy, angry, hormonal tween beasts.

When my son entered middle school, we sat him down to have the puberty talk. It went something like this.

ME: Son, you are entering puberty.

SON: I know, mom. We watched a movie.

ME: You are going to experience some things. Hair will grow in places. (*I look down and make a nodding gesture at his downstairs parts.*)

SON: Mom, stop. I know all of this.

ME: You know all of it. Okay. Let's talk about erections.

SON: MOM! STOP.

ME: All right. If you have any questions, please come talk to me or your father.

Eventually, my husband had a much more in-depth chat with him and he knows I am here to talk about any and all of the things. But boy oh boy, puberty is so awkward and uncomfortable, yet we have to talk with our children about these things. I try to use humor to make it less awful, but it's important that our kids know they can come to us. I don't want any of my kids to think girls get pregnant from a toilet seat, or that the pull-out method works. My third child is distinct proof that it clearly doesn't work.

Puberty causes massive amounts of grief, but like the rest of the stuff we have talked about, it is a phase. One of the phases, in a string of many phases, that makes up childhood and adolescence. Our job is to do what we can to prepare, manage drama and crises, and put out fires. There will be times when you are having a fantastic conversation with your preteen daughter about school. You will think that conversation is going well, but a left turn occurs and now your daughter hates you, hates her life, and never, ever wants to talk to you again, due to the fact that you have single-handedly ruined everything for her in perpetuity.

Remember it is JUST a phase, but also remember another phase is right around the corner. It keeps us on our toes and makes things interesting. Life would be boring if once we got the hang of it, that was it. I was in the car talking with my son after school a while back, and I asked him how things were going. I had gotten wind from another parent that my son was smitten with a girl in his class. I started asking questions about this girl and he said, "I want to ask her for her phone number." My heart stopped. Literally stopped. I started to sweat. *He wants her phone number? Why? Why on earth would he want her phone number?* It dawned on me that at some point my son would in fact have a serious relationship with a girl. He would want to be intimate with this girl. SON OF A BITCH!!!! This parenting thing is no joke.

GETTING "LOVE SHUNNED" BY YOUR KID

The day will come. You will go to grab your child's hand and he will pull away. It feels like a knife in the back, but it is part of the process. When my oldest went into middle school, the rules of the game changed. I dropped him off at school and rolled down the window to say good-bye and he walked right past. He didn't turn around and wave. He didn't say, "I love you too." He just walked away. In that moment, I felt invisible. The little boy who loved to hold my hand was now embarrassed by my presence. I had been officially "love shunned." What did this mean for the future? Was my tweenager going to forget me? Was he going to forget all that I had done for him? Was I no longer going to be the most important lady in his life?

I quickly came to the conclusion that I had failed as a mother. I could hear the voice of Beverly Goldberg in my ears. At some point, all of my children were going to leave me and I would shrivel up and die. They would probably spit on my grave. Those ungrateful sons of bitches. They didn't appreciate anything. I had given my life for them and now they walk away from me, no hugs, no good-byes, no nothing. How dare they! I could have been a lawyer!!!

Well, that got out of control quickly, didn't it? From the moment I pulled away from the middle school, all of those thoughts went rushing through my brain. Luckily, I realized I was being illogical and that middle school is really hard and awkward, and no one wants anything to do with their parents when they are in public at this age. Just having parents is embarrassing. Having me as a mother was epically embarrassing.

I found myself back in the parent pickup line around four o'clock that afternoon. My son got into the minivan. He said hi. I said hi. We sat in silence for a few minutes. I couldn't take it any longer. I finally said, "You love shunned me this morning." He said, "What?" I said, "You love shunned me. I rolled down the window to say good-bye and I said 'I love you' and you walked right past me. You didn't stop. You didn't wave. You just walked away." I was doing my best to keep it together, as he sat quietly in the backseat. He said, "I'm sorry, mom. It's just embarrassing." I knew it was embarrassing, but I still wanted an "I love you." I said, "How about this. How about we say 'I love you' in the car and we just wave at drop-off? Will that work?" I needed him to know that I understood he was growing up, but I still needed to know he loved me. "Sure, mom, that will work."

As our kids grow up they will need us less. It is the goal, isn't it? Our job is to equip them with the tools to become self-sufficient. I, however, still need to hear "I love you." That will never get old. I am doing my best to learn about the space my kids need as they enter the teenage phase of life. I'm sure some of my kids will need more or less space. We will cross that bridge when we get there. Just know that when you are "love shunned," you aren't alone. It is part of the parenting journey. It is necessary for our kids and for us. I'm not exactly sure what an empty nest will feel like, but I know it will mean I was successful. Right now, I just want to do what I can to make sure my kids are ready to fly the coop but want to visit the nest every now and again.

YOU WANT TO DATE? WHAT? I'M DEAD.

If you thought getting "love shunned" was rough, wait until your kid tells you they want to date. I once again found myself in the parent pickup line of the middle school. I opened the minivan door and in jumped my son.

ME: Hey, buddy. How was your day?

SON: Good.

ME: Do you have homework? Did you see any of your friends today? Any pretty girls? (*I asked about the girls as a joke. I like jokes. This one backfired on me.*)

SON: Yeah, I have math homework. I also asked a girl for her phone number.

ME: (*Complete and utter panic spread through my body. I began to sweat. My vision was blurry. I am pretty sure my heart rate escalated to 185 BPM and I may have started my next sentence with a slur.*) PPPPPPHHHH-HOOOOONNNNEEEE number? You asked a girl for her phone number?

SON: Yeah. I like her.

ME: (*Oh, for fuck's sake! I sat there for a minute before I spoke.*) That's nice. I would love to know more about her. You know the rules. Your dad and I will look at your phone if we see fit, so don't say anything you wouldn't want us to see.

SON: I know.

I continued to drive, although I am not sure how I made it home. I was thinking about how my tiny little baby was ready to venture out into the Wild West. Dating? He likes a girl? FUCK! I kept my cool until I got home and spoke to my husband. I began to talk about how he was too young to date. I was going on and on about how this was too soon, it was too sudden, and how we should probably intervene. My husband smiled and laughed. "He is 13. It is normal that he likes girls. He is supposed to date. Why do you think he takes three showers a day?"

An audible gasp left my mouth. "Shut up. He is only in seventh grade."

Later that night we sat him down and talked about what it meant to date. We discussed consent and how to be a gentleman. We discussed what "No" means and we talked about his priorities. I am sure it was super awkward for him, because parts of me didn't want to be involved in the conversation either, but we needed to have it.

Later that week we went shopping for Valentine's Day cards for our kids' classes. My son asked me if he could buy his new friend a gift. He picked out a stuffed llama and some chocolates. *Turn the knife, kid, keep turning that knife.* The next morning he took all of her gifts into school with him. When he got home, I asked him if she liked them; he replied, "Yes." Nothing more, nothing less. He didn't give me any details.

Their relationship lasted a few more weeks. One day he came home and I asked how things were going with her. His eyes began to well up with tears. He said, "She said she likes someone else. She doesn't like me anymore." I did everything I could to prevent myself from crying. This trampy-ass tween of a hussy just trashed my beautiful little boy's heart. Who on earth did she think she was? Seriously? How could she not understand what a catch my son was?

It was in that moment that I understood part of why my mother-in-law dislikes me. No woman will ever be good enough for our sons. I really hope that isn't true. I hope that one day I will have a fantastic relationship with whoever my son marries. After doing my best to make my son feel better, I went to tell my husband what happened. I called this poor girl every nasty name in the book. I truly have no idea about this girl. She is most likely a very nice girl. She is only 13, for crying out loud. But in that moment, I needed to vilify her to make myself feel better. Luckily, I didn't say any of the things I was thinking to my son. I told him that dating can be tough and people can change their minds. You might like one person today, and like someone else tomorrow. I gave him the whole "there are so many fish in the sea" chat and moved on. A few days later, he was back to himself. His road will most likely be paved with broken hearts, but I had no idea, until that moment, that I will most likely suffer a broken heart right alongside each of my children, each and every time it happens to them. This parenting thing can be a real bitch, can't it?

MY DIVA DAUGHTER, THE FRENCHWOMAN

Growing up I was a tomboy. I played outside. I built forts. I rode my bike and played soccer until we had to go inside each night. I never brushed my hair; some things never change. I had zero fashion sense. I hate drama. Like, I HATE DRAMA. Fast-forward to the year 2009, when my sweet and spicy daughter Sophia Marie was born. It was the coldest night of the year, which in Florida means it was about 40 degrees. I was so worried that she would freeze that I stuck her inside my bathrobe, and I walked her all night long. She was a tiny little peanut. I was so excited to complete our family. We now had a boy and a girl. Spoiler: our family wasn't complete, but at the time I didn't know that my husband was going to get employee of the month and we were going to have drunken couch sex a year from giving birth, thus having Brian in October of 2010.

Back to sweet Sophia. She was the happiest baby. Like, legit, the happiest baby. She never cried. She slept through the night very early on. She always had a smile on her face. She was amazing . . . that is, until she turned one year old. It was like a light switch went on and she became a complete diva. She would break things, slam doors, and throw tantrums that would rival Lindsay Lohan circa 2013.

She wanted to be independent. She wanted to be the center of attention. I'm pretty sure she wanted to be an only child. By the time Sophia was entering elementary school, she was a full-on fashionista. She would match her outfits. Coordinate bows and jewelry. She got her first makeup kit at age five and started perfecting her "smoky eye" by age six.

Sophia is my child that always knew exactly what she wanted, and she would do just about anything to get it. She was named after Sophia Petrillo, my favorite character on my all-time favorite television show, *The Golden Girls*. I have always been more of a Dorothy, but my sweet Sophia has the mouth of a Sophia Petrillo. One day, I truly hope that she will use that gift for the power of good and not evil.

Sophia entered puberty early. I was a very late bloomer, so when I started to notice some changes in her body, I was surprised. What? Why? How on earth was this happening? I called the pediatrician's office and took her in the next day. I needed a medical professional to talk me off the ledge. After a quick five-minute visit, it was confirmed. My sweet and spicy Sophia was in the throes of puberty.

We left the doctor's office and we went to Target. I needed coffee and retail therapy, and we had to take a walk down the feminine hygiene aisle. We talked about pads and tampons. We talked about breast development and hormones. We talked about our personal space. We talked, and talked, and talked, and then talked some more. Sophia handled it like a complete champ. She said she knew she was having feelings, but wasn't able to control her emotions. I let her in on a secret, I also have trouble controlling my emotions at times, and I understood how she was feeling. I tried to laugh, but I really wanted to cry. We bought a bunch of pretty pink and purple boxes of panty liners and wipes, and went home.

That night I crawled into my closet and cried. My diva daughter was becoming a woman, and although she might be ready for it, I clearly wasn't. I was sitting there trying to figure out how I was even old enough for this. I was still very young, like spring chicken young, and way too vibrant to have a son and now daughter going through puberty. I mean, I was only 38. WAIT. SHIT. I WAS 38! THAT IS CLEARY OLD ENOUGH. FUCK! I quickly got even more depressed and I called for my husband to bring me a bottle of wine and a bag of chocolate to the closet. Soon enough there were going to be boys sniffing around, looking to date my diva daughter. Looking to deflower my diva daughter. At that moment, I made it my mission to make sure that Sophia could handle any situation. I take every opportunity I get to talk about boys, body positivity, the importance of working hard in school, because, you know, brains matter. I make sure to talk to her about how amazing, funny, talented, and smart she is. I want her to know that she is the grand prize. Never, ever the runner-up.

TODAY MY OLDEST WAS A TODDLER AGAIN... AND I FREAKED OUT A LITTLE BIT

Do you ever have those flashback, déjà vu moments? You know, the moments where you look at your kids and you flash back to when they were an infant or a toddler? Well, I vividly remember having one of those moments when my older son was 14, and although it made me happy, it also freaked me out a little bit.

I was walking through the house doing my daily toy, clothing, and food wrapper pickup one day when I saw my older son's blanket. Not a comforter, but his baby blanket. He was a teenager at this point, but he still slept with the Elmo blanket that he got when he was an infant.

That blanket has been through a lot. I'm not sure why it hit me so hard when I saw the blanket, because I see it every day, but that day it hit me in the gut. I saw his blanket sitting there next to his Zelda sheets, which are fitted to his queen mattress. Yes, his queen mattress, because he has hit puberty and is growing like a weed.

His face seems to change almost daily. I catch glimpses of his father sometimes and I giggle. My firstborn is growing up in front of my eyes, and there are days when he is so cranky and puberty-ridden that I can't stand it.

His big emotions take over his middle school body and I just want to reverse time. I want to swaddle him up in his Elmo blanket and go back to when he would crawl up onto my lap.

Another school year has come to an end and the Elmo blanket is one year closer to extinction. I am sure at some point he will stop sleeping with that blanket, but I hope it isn't any-time soon. I love that he still wears that damn thing like a scarf.

Most days are so crazy busy that I usually walk straight past the Elmo blanket and never give it a second thought.

That day I stopped.

I thought about how many times we used to watch *Elmo's World*.

I thought about how he would drag that blanket behind him like Linus from the "Peanuts" gang.

I thought about how cute he looked in overalls when he was two.

I sat and held that Elmo blanket, pretending my son was a toddler.

I cried while holding his Elmo blanket.

With three kids, I live a very go, go, go lifestyle. I rarely sit. I am constantly doing something for someone. I do my best to be in the moment, but moments go so fast now.

I hope to always remember this. The day I stopped and al-lowed my mind to travel to a memory I love—when my oldest was a toddler. It was amazing, even though it freaked me out a little bit.

Is This the End???

I hope you enjoyed reading this book. I hope this book made you feel better about where you are in your parenting journey. For the first eight years of mine, I felt like I was in solitary confinement. I felt like I had to keep all of my racing thoughts, emotions, fears, and parenting failures a secret. I felt like every other mom was doing all of the things that I couldn't. I felt like an overly caffeinated, geriatric hamster, wearing a pair of black leggings, on a treadmill that was stuck on level 9,000. Day in and day out, I was only trying to keep up. I was suffering in silence.

I don't want any parent to feel this way. I want to make sure that the raw, real truths about parenting are brought to light. I want moms to know that they are not alone, and that most every other mom out there can relate. I didn't really understand empathy until I had kids. I never really understood what it meant to be in someone else's shoes. I am the mom who has spent her evenings in the closet crying. I am the mom who has yelled at her kids in public. I am the mom who forgot to pick up her kid at school. I am the mom who was too tired to make dinner, so we had cereal. I am the mom who hates crafts and refuses to sew on a button. I am the mom who loves her kids with every fiber in her body. I am a mom just like you.

It is my professional and personal goal to make sure no mom feels isolated and alone. I will do my absolute best to remain transparent in my parenting and share my journey, so that others can see the realities of motherhood. The longer our society pretends to breed perfect parenting, the longer moms will suffer from isolation and depression. They will play the comparison game. They will feel like they aren't enough. I will do everything in my power to fight against that. This book, and all future books I write, will always be written with an end goal of creating community and acceptance for real, raw, unfiltered motherhood.

Acknowledgments

I would like to thank my husband, Dave, and my three children, Matias, Sophia, and Brian. None of this would have been possible without you. Clearly, it was a book on marriage and motherhood, and you are the material. To my best friends, Eric and Trey, you have been amazingly supportive through this process. I know that having a famous friend can be hard at times, but you'll learn to deal; Trey, I am speaking directly to you. To my Hot Mess Mavens: Julie, Lauri, Jeba, Dana, and Mia, you are amazing. To the entire Hot Mess Express community and all of my friends over on That's Inappropriate and Filter Free Parents. Thank you to my agent Rachel Sussman for talking me off the ledge, many times! I am a handful and you were always there to listen.

About the Author

Meredith Masony is the founder of That's Inappropriate, an online parenting community with more than 4 million followers across social platforms, where members can talk about the parenting experiences they love, hate, and everything in between. Meredith is a former teacher and has spoken at women's and social media conferences, including Dad 2.0, Mom 2.0, and Start Loving You. She is also the author of *Scoop the Poop*. Meredith is married to her best friend, Dave, who is now her business partner. They live in Florida with their three children and two dogs.